my Read and Rhyme BIBLE Storybook

To Teri—you have touched many lives with your kindness,
compassion, and wisdom. May your faith continue to be strong and
your love continue to be deep.
You are my daughter, my friend, my angel.
—C. B.

I'd like to dedicate this book, with all my love, to my husband, Jim,
and my two boys, Andy and Jimmy.
Without them, my life would have no "rhyme or reason."
Because of the precious times we've spent together as a family,
I feel inspired and encouraged to provide fun
and meaningful stories of faith for other families to enjoy.
—C. K.

Visit Tyndale's exciting Web site for kids at www.tyndale.com/kids
TYNDALE is a registered trademark of Tyndale House Publishers, Inc.
Tyndale Kids logo is a trademark of Tyndale House Publishers, Inc.
My Read and Rhyme Bible Storybook
Copyright © 2009 by Crystal Bowman and Cindy Kenney. All rights reserved.
Cover and interior illustrations copyright © 2009 by Christiane Engel. All rights reserved.
Illustrator photograph copyright © by Marko Fuchs. All rights reserved.
Designed by Jacqueline L. Nuñez
Edited by Stephanie Voiland
Unless otherwise indicated, all Scripture quotations are taken from the *Holy Bible*, New Living Translation, copyright © 1996, 2004, 2007 by Tyndale House Foundation. Used by permission of Tyndale House Publishers, Inc., Carol Stream, Illinois 60188. All rights reserved.
Scripture quotations marked NIV are taken from the HOLY BIBLE, NEW INTERNATIONAL VERSION®. NIV®. Copyright © 1973, 1978, 1984 by International Bible Society. Used by permission of Zondervan. All rights reserved.

Library of Congress Cataloging-in-Publication Data
Bowman, Crystal.
My read and rhyme Bible storybook / Crystal Bowman and Cindy Kenney ; illustrated by Christiane Engel.
      p. cm.
   "Tyndale kids."
   Includes indexes.
   ISBN 978-1-4143-2016-8 (hc)
   1. Bible stories, English. I. Kenney, Cindy, date. II. Engel, Christiane. III. Title.
BS551.3.B72 2009
220.9'505--dc22

                              2008051925

Printed in Singapore
15 14 13 12 11 10 09
 7   6   5   4   3   2   1

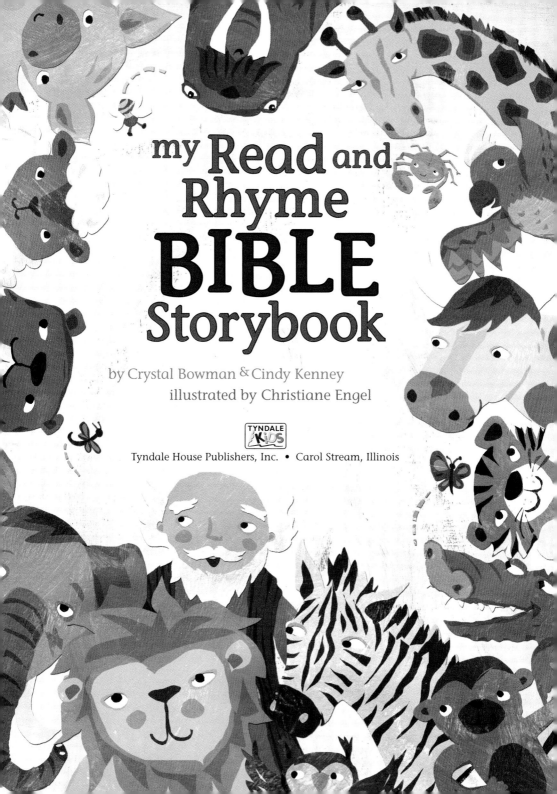

my Read and Rhyme
BIBLE
Storybook

by Crystal Bowman & Cindy Kenney
illustrated by Christiane Engel

TYNDALE KIDS

Tyndale House Publishers, Inc. • Carol Stream, Illinois

Contents

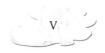

Introduction

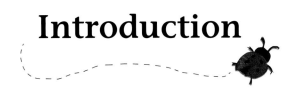

Every parent searches for a Bible that will draw his or her child into God's Word in a fun and engaging manner. Parents are also looking for ways to help their children learn how to read. Because time is precious, we created *My Read and Rhyme Bible Storybook* as a tool to excite and involve children in God's message while also teaching them how to read and rhyme!

My Read and Rhyme Bible Storybook will provide you with great opportunities to connect with your child as you spend time sharing God's Word and take part in fun activities together. Your child will soak in the fascinating messages presented in a fun, new, and unique way. Learning to read has never been so appealing, as children connect the rhymes, observe patterns, and put the words together on their own.

Teachers will find *My Read and Rhyme Bible Storybook* a great resource too. Every story is solidly grounded in the Bible and accurately reflects God's Word with language designed for young readers. Follow-up questions are provided after each story, along with fun, simple activities that everyone will enjoy.

Each Bible story has words for beginning readers to sound out and compre-hend. Short, simple words and sentences allow readers to understand the stories without getting tripped up by concepts that are beyond their reading level. The rhythm and rhymes allow for easy word connections, a fun and whimsical flow, and a positive reading experience.

Each story provides the following tools to enhance the reading experience for children, parents, and teachers alike.

• I Can Learn These Words
Key words and concepts that may be new to beginning readers are introduced at the start of each story. The pronunciations for these words are found before each story as well.

• I Can Say These Names and Places
Children are introduced to key people and places from the Bible at the beginning of each story. The words are broken down into smaller segments to help readers learn how to say each one, and a glossary at the end of the book provides brief descriptions.

• I Can Read These Words
Learning to read is a process of discovery that involves encountering new words and keeping up with familiar ones. At the end of each story are age-appropriate words that children can practice reading and can find in the story.

• I Can Find the Words That Rhyme
Two columns of rhyming words can be found at the end of each story to encourage readers to learn how to rhyme. Children can say each word aloud and then find the words from column one that rhyme with the words in column two. This list also serves as a starting point for readers to come up with additional words of their own that rhyme with each pair.

• I Can Answer These Questions
Each story is followed by questions to help readers comprehend what they've read and apply it to their everyday lives. Some questions are factual, and others encourage readers to think beyond the facts to connect with the story on a personal level.

• I Can Do These Activities
After each story, there are fun activities, games, and crafts that will help readers engage in creative application of the message. Readers can participate in these activities on their own, with a friend or adult, or in a classroom setting.

My Read and Rhyme Bible Storybook is the perfect book to inspire children with God's Word while helping them learn to read and understand rhyme. It also serves as a useful devotional tool, a helpful teaching device, and a wonderful way to connect children with God's messages and with others. Don't wait a minute longer—share this book with your child and have some fun!

Old Testament

God Makes a Big World

GENESIS 1–2

I Can Learn These Words
buzzing (BUZZ-ing)
twinkle (TWINK-ull)
special (SPEH-shull)
holy (HOLE-ee)
blessed (BLEST)

A long time ago
there was nothing at all.
No sand, no lakes,
no bugs that crawl.
No dogs, no fish,
no buzzing bees.
No hills, no grass,
no flowers or trees.

But God was there.
He knew what to do.
He said, "It is time
to make something new.
I'll make a big world.
I'll start right away."
And so God made
the very first day.

God said to the dark,
"Let there be light!"
The light he called day.
The dark he called night.
God liked what he did,
for it was just right.

The next day God made
the earth and the sky.
The earth was down low.
The sky was up high.
The sky was big.
The sky was blue.
That's what God did
on day number two.

The next day God made
the land and the seas.
He made the grass,
the flowers and trees.
God said to himself,
"I like what I see."
That's what God did
on day number three.

The fourth day God made
the sun and the moon.
The moon shone at night.
The sun shone at noon.
He made pretty stars
to twinkle and glow.
God said the words,
and then it was so.

6

The fifth day God made
the birds in the air
and fish in the sea,
so they could swim there.
God looked all around
at the skies and the shore.
He said, "This is good!
But I want to do more."

The sixth day God made
something else that was grand!
He made the animals
to live on the land.
Some could run fast,
and others could crawl.
But this you should know—
that God made them all!

7

And then God said,
"I like what I see!
But I want some people
to spend time with me."
So God took some dust
right from the land.
He held it closely
and breathed in his hand.
Then God made a man
and a woman, too.
And then his work
was finally through.

God looked around
at the end of the day.
The world was good
in every way.

God did not work
on day number seven.
God took a rest
that day in heaven.
And it was so,
right from the start.
One special day
was set apart.
The day was holy.
The day was blessed.
The day became
a day of rest.

I Can Read These Words

world
animals
rest

I Can Find the Words That Rhyme

sky	trees
blue	grand
land	high
bees	two

I Can Answer These Questions

How many days did it take God to make the world?

Why do you think God rested on the seventh day? Can you think of times when it is good for you to rest?

I Can Do These Activities

Make a big picture of the world God made. On your picture, write the names of some of the things God made.

Draw a picture of your favorite animal. Color it and cut it out. Write down the name of the animal. Can you move around and make sounds like that animal?

The First Family

GENESIS 2–4

The first man was Adam,
and Eve was his wife.
God wanted to give them
a nice, happy life.
He made a big garden
with rivers and trees.
God said, "Enjoy all
the fruit that you please.
You just can't eat
from the tree in the middle.
Do not take a bite,
not even a little."

One day in the Garden,
a snake came along.
His plan was to make
the people do wrong.
The snake looked at Eve,
and he said with a hiss,
"I know God said no,
but try some of this.
This fruit is delicious.
This fruit makes you wise."
So Eve took a bite.
She believed the snake's lies.

She gave some to Adam,
and what a mistake!
They disobeyed God,
and it made his heart break.
Then Adam and Eve
knew just what they'd done.
They were afraid
and decided to run.

"Where are you?" asked God.
"Did you eat from that tree?
Is that why you both
are hiding from me?"

Adam told God,
"Eve made me eat.
The fruit was so fresh.
It was juicy and sweet."
Eve said to God,
"The snake told a lie.
He said I'd be wise,
so I gave it a try."

God said to the snake,
"You're lower than low.
You'll crawl on your belly
wherever you go."

Then Adam and Eve
were both sent away.
God told them to leave
the Garden that day.
They knew it was wrong
to eat from that tree.
Now Adam and Eve
were as sad as could be.

But Adam and Eve
didn't always stay sad.
God gave them a son,
so then they were glad.
Before very long,
God gave them another.
Their little boy Cain
got a new baby brother.

When Cain grew older,
he planted some seeds.
He cared for the land,
and he picked the weeds.
His brother, Abel,
cared for the sheep.
He watched them eat,
and he watched them sleep.

Then one day Cain
got really mad.
He was so angry
he did something bad.
He hurt his brother,
and his brother died.
Adam and Eve
both cried and cried.

Then God said to Cain,
"Because you've done wrong,
you will move around
for your whole life long.
You must move away
and be on your own."
So Cain left his home
and felt all alone.

Adam and Eve
became very old.
They had many kids,
so we have been told.
Their kids had kids,
and great-grandkids, too.
And so Adam's family
grew and grew.

19

I Can Read These Words

happy
bite
kids

I Can Find the Words That Rhyme

hiss   sweet
eat   told
sad   glad
old   this

I Can Answer These Questions

What names did God give to the first man and woman he
made?

How did the first people God made disobey him? Are there
times when you disobey too?

I Can Do These Activities

Draw a picture of a big garden with fruit trees and flowers and bushes. Make a picture of the tree with the fruit that Adam and Eve were not supposed to eat. Glue pieces of cereal onto the tree to make it look like fruit.

Adam and Eve disobeyed God's rule. Their son Cain also did something very wrong. Read the following lines that talk about doing what is right. If you always obey, pick yes. If you have lots of trouble obeying, pick no. If you are somewhere in the middle, pick sometimes.

- I pick up my toys when my parents ask me to.
  yes   no   sometimes

- I look both ways before crossing the street.
  yes   no   sometimes

- I share with others.
  yes   no   sometimes

- I tell the truth.
  yes   no   sometimes

- I am kind to others.
  yes   no   sometimes

- I listen to my parents.
  yes   no   sometimes

Talk about your answers with a grown-up. Why do you think it is hard for us to do what is right all the time? How does it make God feel when you do something wrong? How can you make God happy?

Noah Builds an Ark

GENESIS 6–9

I Can Learn These Words
ark (ARK)
creatures (CREE-churs)
howling (HOW-ling)
rainbow (RANE-bo)

I Can Say This Name
Noah (NO-uh)

God looked at all the people.
They were mean and they did wrong—
except a man named Noah.
His love for God was strong.
So God said, "Hello, Noah!
I have a job for you.
Build an ark, a big, big ark,
to hold a big, big crew."

God told Noah he was sad.
"My people turned away.
They don't listen to my words.
They never will obey.
I'll send some rain to flood the earth.
But I'll take care of you.
You'll put your family on that boat
and lots of animals, too."

Bang, bang went his hammer,
as Noah built the boat.
The boat grew big, then bigger—
big enough to float.
The people laughed and stared.
They did not understand
how a boat could ever float
upon the dry, dry land.

24

25

God called creatures, big and small,
and birds up in the sky.
Then two by two, they crawled or marched
or flew from way up high.
Buzzing, chirping, growling,
and cock-a-doodle—bark!
Oinking, mooing, howling—
all heard upon that ark.

The door was closed and thunder boomed!
Then pitter, pitter, pat,
it rained upon the earth below.
Can you imagine that?
For forty days and forty nights,
the rain came down, down, down!
Drip, drop, splash! It rained and poured
and covered the whole town.

"Quack!" said the ducks. The cats meowed
from on their floating ride.
"Buzzz!" "Cuckoo!" "Peep, peep!" and "Baaa!"
They all stayed dry inside.
But Noah and his family
cared for everyone.
As lions roared and gators snapped,
their work was never done.

Suddenly, the rain just stopped!
The sun shone in the sky!
A dove flew out but then came back,
for nothing yet was dry.
They waited and they waited,
then they sent the bird again.
It found a branch and brought it back.
The earth was dry by then.

Soon all around the land appeared.
Everyone gave a cheer!
A rainbow shone up in the sky,
and God said, "Do not fear.
I'll never flood the earth again.
The rainbow is a sign.
Think about my promise
each time these colors shine."

I Can Read These Words

build
birds
rain

I Can Find the Words That Rhyme

shine   cheer
that   float
fear   sign
boat   pat

I Can Answer These Questions

Why do you think God saved Noah, his family, and two of each kind of animal?

What sign did God give to help Noah remember his promise? What are some other promises God makes to all of us?

I Can Do These Activities

Cut a paper plate in half to make a rainbow. Color it with each color in the rainbow. Starting at the top of the plate, make curved lines about one half inch apart. Color in each area from the top down to make the rainbow colors: red, orange, yellow, green, blue, and purple. Practice writing the name of each color. Hang your rainbow up and remember God's promise that he will always take care of us!

Use brown paper lunch bags to create two animal puppets like the ones on Noah's ark. Draw the face on the bottom of each bag. Decorate it with colored paper, cotton balls, yarn, buttons, fabric, or crayons. Think of a name for each animal and write it near the top edge of the bag.

A Tall Tower

GENESIS 11

After the flood,
Noah's family grew.
His sons had some kids,
then they had kids too.
Parents and children
and all kinds of cousins
and uncles and aunts
were there by the dozens.

The people moved east.
And then one day,
they found a good place.
They decided to stay.
"Come on," they said.
"Let's build a city.
We can use bricks
to make it look pretty.

33

"Let's build a tower
that's strong and high.
Let's build a tower
way up to the sky.
The tower will show
how great we are.
We're greater than great!
We're the greatest by far!"

When God looked down,
he shook his head.
"This isn't good!
It's bad!" he said.
"The people will think
they're greater than me.
I must do something.
This cannot be!"

God is much smarter
than a woman or man.
He knew what to do.
He had a great plan.
God mixed up the words
the people would say.
And so they no longer
could talk the same way.
They could not work
or speak to each other
when some talked one way
and some talked another.

Their big, fancy city
was still very small.
The tower they started
was not very tall.
And so they all learned
God's the greatest of all.

They left the city.
They left the tower.
Their plans fell apart
because of God's power.
God wanted the people
to move far away.
That is what happened
the very same day.

Some people went east.
Some people went west.
They all found out
that God knows what's best.

I Can Read These Words

city
bricks
tower

I Can Find the Words That Rhyme

too	power
tall	man
plan	grew
tower	all

I Can Answer These Questions

What did the people want to build? Why didn't God want them to build it?

How did God let them know that nobody can be as great as he is? How does it make you feel that God is the best?

I Can Do These Activities

When the people started speaking different words, no one could understand each other! See if you can make up some silly words, like "gleeb" and "miffer." Write them on a piece of paper just for fun. What might they mean?

Find some blocks, empty boxes, cans, or other fun items to build a tower. You may also use things like marshmallows and toothpicks, playing cards, or crackers with cheese spread. How high can you make your tower?

Abraham
Trusts God

GENESIS 12, 15–18, 21–22

I Can Learn These Words
fireflies (FI-er-flize)
adore (uh-DOOR)
amazing (uh-MAZE-ing)
deserts (DEZZ-erts)
worshiped (WERE-shipt)

I Can Say These Names
Abraham (ABE-ruh-ham)
Sarah (SAIR-uh)
Isaac (EYE-zick)

"Abraham!"
God said one day.
"Leave this land.
Go where I say."
Abraham
went right away.
He trusted God
that very day.

God led the way
to the new land.
And then God said,
"Here's what I've planned.
Abraham,
someday you'll be
the father of
a big family!"

Abraham
still trusted God.
So he believed
and gave a nod.
But Sarah asked,
"How can this be?
No child's been born
to you and me!"
They had no kids,
and yet they knew
God's promises
are always true.

The years went by,
and they grew old.
No children yet
for them to hold.

"Abraham!"
God said one night.
"Look at the stars,
all shining bright!"
And so he looked
into the sky.
He saw so many
stars up high!
"Count each one
like fireflies,
for that will be
your family's size."

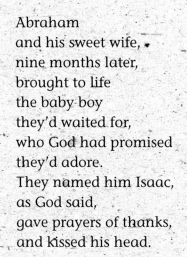

Abraham
and his sweet wife,
nine months later,
brought to life
the baby boy
they'd waited for,
who God had promised
they'd adore.
They named him Isaac,
as God said,
gave prayers of thanks,
and kissed his head.

As Isaac grew
his parents shared
about God's love
and how God cared.
They loved him so.
He brought them joy.
They were so pleased
to have their boy.

And then—a test.
God came to say,
"Abraham,
will you obey?
Show me your love,
and this is how:
give Isaac back,
and do it now."
Abraham
was feeling low
but trusted God
and said he'd go.

Dad and son
climbed way up high
a mountain top
to say good-bye.
But then God said,
"Now I can see
how much you love
and trust in me.
This brings me such
amazing joy!
So you may keep
your special boy."

"I will bless you.
You will see
how many children
there will be—
more than the stars
up in the sky,
or grains of sand
in deserts dry.
All the nations
will be blessed
because you have
just passed this test."

Abraham
and Isaac, too,
worshiped God
because they knew
that God is good—
his love is true.
Believe in God,
for he loves you!

I Can Read These Words

land
stars
trust

I Can Find the Words That Rhyme

boy   you
go   now
true   low
how   joy

I Can Answer These Questions

How did Abraham show he trusted God? What is one way
you can show that you trust God?

Why did Abraham and Isaac worship God?

I Can Do These Activities

Write the word STARS on a piece of black paper. Then carefully use a pencil tip to punch tiny holes through the paper where the letters are. Hold the paper up to a light to see your word spelled out against the black "sky"!

Draw three happy faces and write the names ABRAHAM, SARAH, and ISAAC below them. Then fill your paper with happy faces to show Abraham's grandchildren, great-grandchildren, and many children after that!

Twin Brothers

GENESIS 25; 27; 29

I Can Learn These Words
starving (STARVE-ing)
blessing (BLESS-ing)
birthright (BIRTH-rite)

I Can Say These Names
Rebekah (ruh-BECK-uh)
Esau (EE-saw)
Jacob (JAY-cub)

Rebekah and Isaac
wanted a son.
God gave them two
instead of just one.
The first baby boy
was hairy and red.
"We'll call him Esau,"
his mom and dad said.
His brother came next.
He was holding on tight.
They named him Jacob.
It sounded just right.

When Esau grew up,
he hunted for meat.
He brought back some food
for his family to eat.
When Jacob grew up,
he liked the indoors.
He stayed by his mom
and helped with the chores.

Then one day Jacob
was cooking some stew.
Esau came home.
He wanted some too.
"I'm starving!" said Esau.
"Give me a bite!"
But Jacob did something
that just wasn't right.

"Make me a promise,"
said Jacob that day.
"Make me a promise
right now, right away.
Give me the blessing
that Dad planned for you.
Give me your birthright.
I'll give you my stew."

Esau cried out,
"It's food that I need.
What good are words?"
So Esau agreed.
He traded his blessing
for soup and for bread.
He couldn't take back
the words that he'd said.

The days and the months
and the years passed by.
Isaac was old.
He was ready to die.
He said to Esau,
"Please go and find
some meat we can eat,
the very best kind.
When you come back,
here's what I'll do:
I'll give you a blessing.
It's only for you."

While Esau was gone,
Jacob was sly.
He went to his father
and told a bad lie.
Old Isaac's eyes
couldn't see very well.
This son wasn't Esau,
but he couldn't tell.
"I'm Esau," said Jacob.
"Here is your meat.
Give me my blessing
after you eat."

So Isaac ate,
then he blessed his son.
But he didn't know
he blessed the wrong one.

When Esau came home,
he quickly found out
what Jacob had done.
He let out a shout.
"Bless me, my father!
Please bless me, too!"
But Isaac cried out,
"Oh, what can I do?
Your brother tricked me.
I blessed him instead."
Then Esau was angry.
"I hate him!" he said.

Rebekah told Jacob,
"Go far away.
Run to your uncle.
That's where you must stay."
So Jacob moved far
from Esau, his brother.
He left his home,
his father and mother.
He worked for his uncle.
He soon found a wife.
And God was with him
the rest of his life.

I Can Read These Words

son
brother
bless

I Can Find the Words That Rhyme

red	sly
brother	mother
lie	kind
find	said

I Can Answer These Questions

How were Jacob and Esau different from each other? What did each brother like to do?

Why did Jacob have to go far away? How would you feel if you went somewhere far away?

I Can Do These Activities

Create a big pot of "word stew." Get a big pot from the kitchen. Write ten words on different pieces of paper and put them in the pot. Pull the words out of the pot and see if you can make a sentence. Play it again with ten different words.

Draw a picture of the people in your family and color it. Be sure to include yourself in the picture. Use black, red, yellow, or brown yarn or ribbon to make hair for the people in your picture. Then make a list of words that describe each person. Think of something good to say about everyone.

Joseph and His Brothers

GENESIS 37; 39–47

I Can Learn These Words
traders (TRADE-ers)
surprise (suh-PRIZE)
forgive (for-GIVE)

I Can Say This Name
Joseph (JOE-seff)

I Can Say This Place
Egypt (EE-jipt)

Jacob had twelve sons,
but one he loved the best.
Joseph was his name.
He was so very blessed.
Jacob gave his son
a special coat one day.
Joseph was so proud.
He shouted, "Hip hooray!"

Joseph had a dream
about a bunch of wheat.
His brothers all bowed down
in front of Joseph's feet.
Then he dreamed of stars
and moonlight shining bright.
Eleven stars bowed down
in front of him that night.

When Joseph shared his dreams,
his brothers got so mad.
"He thinks he'll be our king!"
his brothers told their dad.

One day Joseph's brothers
were caring for their sheep.
They tossed their brother Joseph
into a well so deep.
Some traders came along.
His brothers gave a wave.
They sold their little brother,
so Joe became a slave.

The brothers traveled home,
wondering what to do.
They told their dad, "A lion came!
Here's Joe's coat for you."

Their dad was very sad.
For many days he cried.
He thought that it was true.
He didn't know they'd lied.

Joseph worked in Egypt.
He worked hard all day long,
until a woman lied
and said that he did wrong.
They put him in a jail,
but Joseph did not fight.
He knew by trusting God
that things would be all right.

The king had odd dreams too.
He said, "I worry so!
Who knows what my dreams mean?
Please tell me if you know!"
So Joseph met the king
and left the jail that day.
He said, "The Lord has told me
just what I need to say.
For seven years you'll have
a lot of bread and meat.
For seven years that follow,
you'll have no food to eat."

The king said, "Joe, you're wise.
Come and work for me.
You'll be a mighty leader."
So Joseph did agree.
He worked for seven years,
piling food up high.
Then people came to Joseph.
They needed his supply.

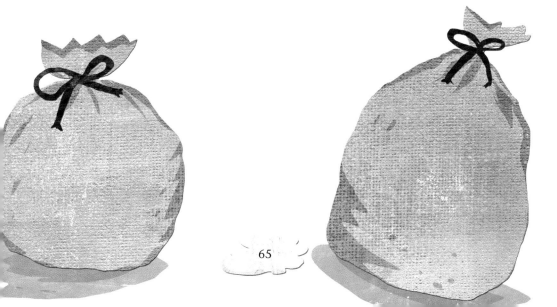

Joe's brothers came to Egypt.
They had no food to eat.
They didn't know their brother Joe
was who they soon would meet.
When Joseph stood before them,
they bowed down to the floor.
Their brother looked much different
than many years before.

Joseph knew his brothers
but did not say a thing.
He gave his brothers lots of food
to last them through the spring.
When the spring was over,
Joe's brothers needed more.
They came to beg from Joseph
and bowed down on the floor.

"I'm your brother Joseph,"
he said to their surprise.
And they could not believe
he was right before their eyes.
Joseph said, "God had a plan.
He is very wise.
You're my brothers. I'm not mad.
I forgive you guys."

Joseph told his brothers,
"Come here and live with me."
So they packed up their things
and joined his family.

I Can Read These Words

coat
dreams
food

I Can Find the Words That Rhyme

feet	do
night	bright
hooray	wheat
you	day

I Can Answer These Questions

What were some things that went wrong for Joseph? Why did he trust in God when things went wrong?

What did Joseph do when he saw his brothers again at the end of the story? What do you think you would have done?

I Can Do These Activities

The story of Joseph is about the good things that can happen when you forgive someone. Use a big piece of paper to create your own story that shows something good that happens when you forgive someone. Tell your story with words you know and with pictures you draw.

Play a fun spelling game. See how many words from the story you can draw a picture of. Then try to spell those words without looking at the story. If you can spell the word, toss a ball or crumpled-up piece of used paper into a trash can. You get one point for the correct spelling and one point for getting a basket. See how you score!

Baby Moses

EXODUS 2

I Can Learn These Words
command (come-AND)
princess (PRIN-sess)
palace (PAL-us)

I Can Say These Names
Hebrew (HE-brew)
Moses (MO-ziss)

I Can Say This Place
Israel (IZ-ree-ul)

The new king of Egypt
was very mean—
the meanest king
you've ever seen!
The people of Israel
lived in his land.
Since he did not like them,
he gave a command.

"Make them our slaves!"
the king said one day.
"Get all Hebrew boys
out of my way.
I don't want them here!
They all have to go!
I am the king,
and it will be so!"

During that time,
a man and his wife
were blessed with a boy,
a tiny new life.
His mother kept him
hidden inside.
But soon her baby
was too big to hide.

She made a basket
from tar and from reeds,
to float in the river
among the tall weeds.
The sweet baby boy
stayed safe and dry
as his sister watched
from the bushes nearby.

Along came a princess,
the evil king's daughter.
She found the basket
floating on the water.
She saw the baby
and held him so tight.
"Don't cry," she said.
"I'll make things all right."

The baby's sister
ran over to say,
"Do you need a nanny?
I'll find one today."
"Yes," said the princess.
"Please do not delay."

The sister ran home
to find her mother.
Then they ran back
to get her brother.
The princess said,
"Here is your fee.
When he is older,
bring him to me."

The mom loved her son,
and she watched him grow.
But soon it was time
to let her son go.
The princess was happy
the day that he came.
She said, "You are Moses.
That's your new name."

As Moses grew up,
God's people were sad.
They worked hard as slaves.
This made Moses mad.
He tried to help them
but hurt them instead.
The king told his helpers,
"I want Moses dead!"

So Moses went out
of the palace that day.
He ran to the desert
far, far away.

I Can Read These Words

king
slaves
name

I Can Find the Words That Rhyme

mean	reeds
hide	inside
weeds	water
daughter	seen

I Can Answer These Questions

Who found the baby floating in a basket?

Why did the baby get to go back home with his mother
and sister? How would you feel if you were the baby's
brother or sister and he got to come home with you again
for a while?

I Can Do These Activities

Using a brown bag or brown paper, draw a basket and cut
it out. On a piece of plain, heavy paper, draw a river along
the length of the paper. Then draw a picture of baby
Moses. Glue the basket onto the paper so Moses is inside

the basket and the basket is floating in the river. Next, draw a picture of the baby's sister beside the river. Now cut pieces of tall grass from green paper, or find pieces of real grass to glue along the water. Put some grass in front of Moses' sister to help her hide. If you can find some small leaves or sand, glue that onto the picture as well.

The baby's sister was watching over Moses, but God was watching over both of them. He watches over you, too. Write these words on the bottom of your picture:

GOD WATCHES OVER ME WHEN I _____.

Think about all the things you do. How many different words can you use to finish the sentence? Make a list of those words and then write one of them on the blank line.

Find a friend or a family member to play the game "I Spy" with you. Take turns letting one person spot something you can both see. That person will say, "I spy something [insert color clue]." For example, if you see an apple, you might say, "I spy something red!" The other player tries to guess what the item is by asking yes or no questions. When the person guesses the item, let him or her find an object and you do the guessing.

After each player has had a few turns, talk about things you might "spy" that show people are in need of some sort of help. For example, "I spy a little sister who needs help tying her shoe." Then talk about things you can do for people who may need your help.

Moses Leads
God's People

EXODUS 3–15

I Can Learn These Words
plagues (PLAYGZ)
finally (FINE-uh-lee)
soldiers (SOLE-jers)
straight (STRATE)

I Can Say This Name
Egyptians (ee-JIP-shuns)

Moses found work
in the desert to do.
Then something happened—
amazing but true.
He saw a bush.
The bush was on fire.
It didn't burn up.
The flames went much higher.

"Moses! Moses!"
he heard someone say.
"Take off your shoes
and stand far away.
I am the Lord.
Do not come near.
This ground is holy,
but please do not fear.

"My people are sad.
I've heard their cries.
You're going to Egypt.
I'll help you be wise."

So Moses went back
to Egypt's land.
He said to the king,
"Here's God's command:
'You must let all
my people go.'"
The king shook his head.
The king said, "No!"

Then God sent plagues
of frogs and flies.
The cows fell dead
before their eyes.
The water turned red.
Small bugs flew around.
A plague of big bugs
covered the ground.
Hail pounded down.
Darkness came too.
God sent ten plagues
before he was through.

The king finally cried,
"I've had enough!
Get out of here
and take your stuff!"
God's people left
that very night.
A cloud of fire
gave them some light.
They hurried up.
They could not wait.
But that mean king
was filled with hate.

All of a sudden
the king said, "No!
I've changed my mind.
You cannot go!"

He called his soldiers:
"Come follow me!
They're getting away.
This cannot be!
Hop on your horses.
Pick up the pace!"
So the king's army
joined in the chase.
All the Egyptians
looked up ahead.
"At last we've caught them!"
the evil king said.

The people cried out
to Moses in fear.
"Why in the world
did you bring us here?"
Then Moses told them,
"You won't have to fight.
The Lord your God
will save you tonight."

God said to Moses,
"Hold your staff high.
I'll make a pathway
so you can pass by."
So Moses raised
his arms out straight.
Then God did something
very great!

The waters spread out
so far and wide.
The people marched
to the other side.
God made a path
right through the sea.
And all God's people
soon were free.
God's people cheered
and started to pray,
"Thank you, God!
You saved us today!"

I Can Read These Words

bush
shoes
free

I Can Find the Words That Rhyme

fire   eyes
flies   today
pace   higher
pray   chase

I Can Answer These Questions

How many plagues did God send to the people in Egypt?
Can you name some of them and write them down on a
piece of paper?

How do you think God's people felt when they were leaving
Egypt?

I Can Do These Activities

God's people had to wait many, many years for God to send someone to lead them out of Egypt. Sometimes we have to wait for things too. Here is a list of some things that are hard to wait for. On a piece of paper, write down the ones that you think are hard to wait for. Put a star by the ones you think are extra hard to wait for.

recess

dinner

your birthday

Christmas

vacation

summer

a party

a visit from a friend

your favorite TV show

time to go out and play

Moses had a big job to do! He had to tell the king of Egypt that God wanted him to let his people go free. What would you say to the king if you were Moses? Write those words on a big sign. Decorate the sign and hang it up where everyone in your family can see it.

The Ten Commandments

EXODUS 20

The Ten Commandments God gave out
were not just rules but all about
his love and keeping us from sin.
So here they are—now let's begin!

God's first command you must obey:
Other gods are not okay!
Worship God in heaven above.
He's the one that you should love.

God's second command you must obey:
Do not bow and do not pray
to anyone except the Lord.
All other gods must be ignored.

89

God's third command you must obey:
Respect God's name. Watch what you say.
Don't use it any way that's wrong.
Show God your love your whole life long.

God's fourth command you must obey:
Worship on the Sabbath day.
Take the time to hear God's story.
Praise and thank him. Give him glory.

God's fifth command you must obey:
Show respect. Do it this way.
Honor your parents in all you do.
Help them out and listen, too.

God's sixth command you must obey.
Keep it in mind. Tuck it away.
Do not kill or hurt another.
Just be kind and love each other.

God's seventh command you must obey
if you choose to marry someday:
When a husband and wife say, "I do,"
their love should always be strong and true.

God's eighth command you must obey:
Keep it in your heart to stay.
Do not steal. Don't be unfair.
Share with others and show you care.

God's ninth command you must obey:
Don't tell lies. It's not okay.
Tell the truth, and do what's right.
This is pleasing in God's sight.

God's tenth command you must obey:
Be kind to people every day.
Do not wish for what is theirs.
Instead, include them in your prayers.

God gave commands to show his love,
to lead and guide us from above.
Always listen. Do what's right.
God will help you, day and night.

I Can Read These Words

sin
obey
kind

I Can Find the Words That Rhyme

wrong   sight
care   glory
right   unfair
story   long

I Can Answer These Questions

Which of the commandments are about loving God?

Which of the commandments are about loving others?

I Can Do These Activities

God gave us ten commandments that we should obey. One by one, try to memorize them. As you learn them, practice spelling out the numbers from one through ten. Then create flash cards so that you can teach others to spell numbers. Write each number on a note card. Then choose a simple object and draw the same amount of them as the number on the card. Finish by coloring the objects.

Think of things you can do to show you will obey God's Ten Commandments. Then try to write ten sentences that all begin with:

I will _____ .

Big Walls Fall Down

DEUTERONOMY 34;
JOSHUA 1; 3; 6

I Can Learn These Words
single (SING-gull)
wander (WAND-er)
battles (BAT-ulls)

I Can Say This Name
Joshua (JAH-shoo-uh)

I Can Say These Places
Jordan (JOR-dun)
Jericho (JAIR-uh-ko)

Moses lived a long, long time
before he finally died.
The people were so very sad.
For thirty days they cried.
But God did not forget them.
He always has a plan.
He gave them a new leader.
Joshua was the man.

Joshua was very brave,
for God was on his side.
He led the people straight across
a river deep and wide.

They crossed the Jordan River.
Now that was hard to do!
But God was with them all the way.
He helped them walk right through!

They came up to a city
with big walls up and down.
The Lord God said to Joshua,
"I'm giving you this town."
The city's name was Jericho.
The gates were locked up tight.
God said, "You'll get this city
without a single fight.
Listen to me, Joshua.
Do everything I say.
March around the city once,
and then just walk away.

"For six days you must do this.
But on day number seven,
march around it seven times.
Then give a shout to heaven."
Joshua told the people,
"God's giving us this land.
It's time for us to trust him
and do what he has planned.
No longer will we wander
among the rocks and dust.
God will do great things for us
if we will only trust."

Joshua gave the orders:
"Get ready, here we go!
One-and-two-and-three-and-four!
Now march it, row by row!"

The leaders blew their trumpets.
That's all the people heard.
They marched around the city once
and didn't say a word.

Again the people did this.
For six days in a row,
they marched around the city
as they heard the trumpets blow.

Then it was the seventh day.
The march began once more.
Seven times they marched around,
not like the days before.

The trumpets gave a mighty blast.
God's people gave a shout.
The people in the city
were filled with fear and doubt.

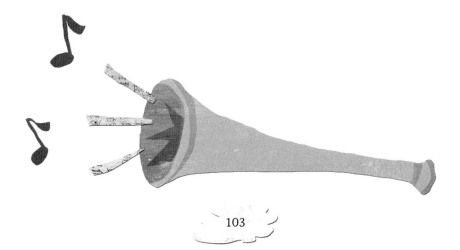

Rumble, rumble. Crash! Boom! Bang!
The noises filled the town!
By God's amazing power,
the walls came crashing down.

God's people took the city.
They shouted with great pride,
"We always win our battles
when God is on our side!"

The people learned to listen
when God said what to do.
They learned that God would help them
and that his words are true.

I Can Read These Words

walls
march
trumpets

I Can Find the Words That Rhyme

fight   trust
seven   tight
dust   heaven
blow   row

I Can Answer These Questions

How many days did the people march around the city?
What was different about the last day?

Why do you think God told the people to march around
the city and shout instead of fight?

I Can Do These Activities

Choose a couch or a big chair in your house and pretend it is the city of Jericho. March around it seven times and don't say a word. After the seventh time, say "Hip hip hooray!" Then say thank you to God for taking care of his people and for taking care of you.

God helped Joshua win the battle against Jericho without even fighting. God can help you solve your problems too—without fighting. Read the list below and think of ways you can handle your problems without fighting.

What can you do if
• someone teases you at school or on the playground?
• someone breaks your toy?
• there is only one cookie left and two people want it?
• your parents tell you to go to bed and you want to stay up?
• your friend borrows your ball or game and forgets to give it back?

Say a prayer and ask God to help you handle your problems without fighting. Using words you know, write your prayer on a piece of paper that you can keep in your room.

God Sends Gideon

JUDGES 6–8

I Can Learn These Words
enemies (EN-uh-meez)
lesson (LESS-un)
prophet (PRAH-fet)
angel (AIN-jel)

I Can Say This Name
Gideon (GID-ee-un)

I Can Say This Place
Midian (MID-ee-un)

God's people were not listening.
They never would obey.
And so God said bad things would come
to show that's not okay.
For seven years, they planted crops.
But all their crops were smashed.
Their enemies were mean to them,
and all their land was trashed.
And so the people called to God,
"Oh Lord, please hear our prayer!
We've learned our lesson—won't you help?
And show us you still care?"

And so God chose a prophet.
His message was quite clear.
An angel came to Gideon
to calm the prophet's fear.
"God is sending you to help,
and he will make you strong!"
"But I am weak!" said Gideon.
"I fear God may be wrong!"

The angel said, "Don't worry.
You will not be alone.
You will win this battle.
God's power will be shown."

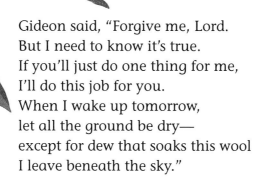

Gideon said, "Forgive me, Lord.
But I need to know it's true.
If you'll just do one thing for me,
I'll do this job for you.
When I wake up tomorrow,
let all the ground be dry—
except for dew that soaks this wool
I leave beneath the sky."

Gideon got up early.
The wool was soaking wet.
Yet all the ground around it
was dry as it could get.
The next night things were different
when Gideon tried again.
He left the wool beneath the sky
to see what would happen then.
Early in the morning,
when Gideon rose from bed,
the wool was dry, but all around
the ground was wet instead.

Gideon knew that God would help.
He called the people near.
He said, "I need some soldiers.
Please come and do not fear!"
God had different plans in mind.
He said, "Too many men!
They'll think they do not need me
and turn from me again.
Before you go to battle
I'll choose which men should fight."
God picked three hundred men in all
to stop the enemies' might.

Gideon told his soldiers,
"God told me what to do.
Listen to my orders—
the Lord will help us through.
Each man must grab a torch and horn
and bottle made of clay.
I'll give you all a special sign.
Then you must shout and play!"

The men got in their places.
Gideon gave the sign.
"For the Lord and Gideon!"
they shouted all in line.
The horns blared out. The bottles crashed.
Their enemies ran in fear.
They won the war because of God
and gave a mighty cheer!

God's people prayed to him for help
against the wicked Midian.
God heard their prayers—he helped them out—
and sent the prophet Gideon.

I Can Read These Words

dew
wool
horn

I Can Find the Words That Rhyme

prayer   again
wet   get
men   clay
play   care

I Can Answer These Questions

How did Gideon and three hundred men win against the strong army of Midian? Why do you think God used only three hundred men to fight against Midian?

Why did God expect his people to listen better and obey his commands after they won the battle? Why does God expect you to obey him?

I Can Do These Activities

Gideon's army used jars made out of clay in their battle against Midian. You can use a jar for this activity too. Clean out a large jar and decorate it with permanent markers and paints, or cover it with glue and tiny tissue paper squares. Write down some words from the story you want to learn and put them into the jar. Each night after dinner or before bed, take three words out of the jar and practice reading them, spelling them, and using them in a sentence.

Gideon listened to God and was a good leader for the Israelites. See how many words you can think of to describe Gideon. Try to choose words that start with as many different letters of the alphabet as you can.

A Very Strong Man

JUDGES 13; 16

I Can Learn These Words
bullies (BULL-eez)
fled (FLED)
cruel (CREW-ull)

I Can Say These Names
Samson (SAM-son)
Delilah (Duh-LIE-luh)

A woman wanted
to have a son.
She didn't have any,
not even one.
God sent an angel
with very good news:
"You'll soon have a son
who God plans to use.
When he grows up,
he will be strong.
Don't cut his hair.
Let it grow long.
Do not drink wine.
Do what I say.
He'll do great things
for God someday."

The woman gave birth
to a baby boy.
The mother's heart
was filled with joy.
She didn't drink wine
or cut the boy's hair.
She was so happy
that God heard her prayer.
She named him Samson.
He grew and grew.
She loved her son
and cared for him too.

Samson became
so big and strong,
just as God knew
he would all along.
The big, mean bullies
came over to fight.
But Samson gave them
quite a fright.
He fought the bullies.
They ran away.
The bullies said,
"We'll get him someday!"

Then Samson went
into the city.
He met a girl
who was so pretty.
She said to Samson,
"My, oh my!
You are so strong.
Please tell me why.
My name's Delilah,
and if you can,
tell me your secret,
you big, strong man!"

Then Samson told
this girl a lie.
"Go find some straps.
They can't be dry.
Tie them around me
until they're tight.
Then I'll be weak.
I'll lose my might."

Delilah did
what Samson said.
But Samson broke
the straps and fled.
Delilah was mad.
"You tricked me!" she cried.
"You made me look silly.
You're mean, and you lied!"

So Samson gave her
another plan.
"Tie me with ropes
as tight as you can."
Delilah obeyed.
She tied him once more.
But Samson broke loose
like he'd done before.

Delilah put braids
in Samson's long hair.
But he was as strong
as a grizzly bear!
Delilah cried out,
"Oh, why can't you see
how silly I feel?
You must not love me!"

Then Samson said,
"I'll tell you why
I am so strong.
This isn't a lie.
My secret is that
my hair is so long.
It hasn't been cut,
so God keeps me strong."

Delilah was glad
she finally found out
what Samson's strength
was all about.
She cut his hair
that very day.
Then God took Samson's
strength away.

I Can Read These Words

strong
baby
big

I Can Find the Words That Rhyme

bear	pretty
fool	cruel
city	hair
along	strong

I Can Answer These Questions

Why was Samson so strong? How strong are you? What makes you strong?

What did Delilah do when she learned the truth about what made Samson strong?

I Can Do These Activities

Draw and color a picture of Samson. Make big muscles on his arms so he looks strong. Glue on long pieces of yarn or ribbon to show his long hair. After you finish your picture, blow up two small balloons and stuff them in your sleeves to make your arms look strong. If you don't have balloons, you can use socks or rags.

Eating good food and getting exercise helps you to be strong. Make a chart to put on the refrigerator. On the chart, make a list of good foods to eat and good ways to exercise. You can use the chart below or make up your own list. Look at the chart every day. Put a check or a sticker by the good foods you eat and the exercises you do.

GOOD FOODS	EXERCISE
apple	walking
banana	riding your bike
orange juice	jumping rope
carrots	roller-skating
oatmeal	doing jumping jacks
chicken	swinging
fish	swimming
beans	doing gymnastics
bread	playing soccer

Ruth's Love and Kindness

RUTH 1–4

I Can Learn These Words
field (FEELD)
replied (ree-PLIDE)

I Can Say These Names
Ruth (ROOTH)
Naomi (Nay-OH-me)
Orpah (OR-puh)
Boaz (BOH-az)

Naomi's sons
each had a wife.
She loved them all
throughout her life.
After ten years,
her sons both died.
Their wives were left
to stay by her side.

They moved away,
but Naomi said,
"Orpah and Ruth,
go home instead.
You two are young.
I'm old and gray.
I'll go on alone—
I'll be okay."

So Orpah left.
But Ruth said, "Never!
I'll stay with you—
always, forever!"

Naomi knew Ruth
would not change her mind.
She said, "My dear,
you are so kind."

Naomi and Ruth
went on their way
and found a place
where they could stay.
Ruth walked into
a field each day
to pick some grain
along the way.
She followed behind
men picking wheat,
catching whatever
she could to eat.

Boaz was kind.
He owned the land.
He asked about Ruth
and what she had planned.
"She lives with Naomi,"
his workers replied.
"Ruth came with her
to be by her side.

"She picks up the grain—
all she can find."
And so Boaz said,
"Leave good grain behind."

Then Boaz told Ruth,
"Stay very near.
Pick up the grain
that you will find here."

Ruth said to Boaz,
"I don't know why
you are so kind
and such a nice guy.
You don't know me.
I'm a stranger to you."
So Boaz answered,
"It's all that you do.
You care for Naomi.
You're lovely and sweet.
The Lord had it planned
that we could meet."

135

Naomi and Ruth
were glad Boaz shared.
They both thanked the Lord
for how much he cared.

Then Boaz asked Ruth,
"Will you be my wife?
I'll care for you
for the rest of your life.
And once we are married,
I'll keep you from harm.
You and Naomi
can live on my farm."

Soon they were married,
and they lived in love,
for God had blessed them
from up above.

I Can Read These Words

grain
nice
kind

I Can Find the Words That Rhyme

never   harm
sweet   guy
farm   meet
why   forever

I Can Answer These Questions

Why do you think Ruth stayed with Naomi?

How did Ruth show love and kindness to Naomi? How did Boaz show love and kindness to Ruth?

Who is someone you can show love and kindness to?

I Can Do These Activities

Learn the words in these verses and read them aloud:

> Jesus replied: "'Love the Lord your God with all your heart and with all your soul and with all your mind.' This is the first and greatest commandment. And the second is like it: 'Love your neighbor as yourself.'" (Matthew 22:37-39, NIV)

Play a game to memorize these verses over the next week or two. Cover two or three words at a time and read the sentences aloud. Keep practicing until you know them by heart!

Make some "kindness coupons." Use heavy paper and write this sentence on each one:
"I will be kind to you by _____."

Fill in the blank with some of the words you've learned in this book or at school. Pass them out to people you want to show love and kindness to.

For example: "I will be kind to you by playing fair." "I will be kind to you by being a good helper."

David and the Giant

1 SAMUEL 17

I Can Learn These Words
shepherd (SHEP-erd)
excuse (ex-KYOOZ)
armor (ARM-er)
sword (SORD)
spear (SPEER)

I Can Say These Names
Goliath (guh-LIE-eth)
David (DAVE-id)

Goliath was a giant,
and he was very mean.
Every day and every night
he always caused a scene.
He said, "Come out and fight me!
Does anybody dare?"
But no one dared to fight him
as he was standing there.

A shepherd boy named David
said, "I will fight this guy!"
The king said, "No, no, no!
I don't want you to try.
You're much too small to fight him.
He'll kill you with one blow."
David said, "Excuse me, sir,
there's something you should know.
I killed a bear and lion.
Oh yes, it is all true.
I know that God will help me
no matter what I do."

The king said, "Go and fight him.
I know you trust the Lord.
But wear my suit of armor,
and take my special sword."

David put the armor on,
then took it off and said,
"This armor is too heavy, sir.
I'll take my sling instead."

David picked up five smooth stones.
He put them in his sack.
He walked up to the giant
and never once turned back.
Goliath looked at David.
Then he began to laugh.
"You come to me with sticks and stones?
I'll break you right in half!"

David said, "You have a spear.
You have a great big sword.
But I have come to fight you
with the power of the Lord.
God will win this battle.
I haven't come alone."
Then David took his sling shot
and put in one small stone.

He threw the stone into the air.
It hit Goliath's head.
Goliath spun around and 'round
before he fell down dead.

The people were so happy
to be alive and free.
The Lord God saved them from
their great big enemy.
The people sang and danced.
They all jumped up and down.
"Hooray, hooray for David—
the bravest man in town!"

David trusted in the Lord.
He knew what God could do.
If you trust God like he did,
then you can be brave too!

David trusted in the Lord.
He knew what God could do.
If you trust God like he did,
then you can be brave too!

I Can Read These Words

giant
stone
brave

I Can Find the Words That Rhyme

dare	stone
sack	there
head	dead
alone	back

I Can Answer These Questions

Why were the people afraid of the giant, Goliath?

Why do you think David was so brave? When can you be brave like David?

I Can Do These Activities

Draw five stones on a piece of paper and cut them out. (Use gray paper, or use white paper and color the stones gray.) Use a dark crayon or marker to write one letter on each stone to spell the word BRAVE. You can also find real stones to use instead of paper. Use markers or paint to write the letters on the stones. If you make the stones out of paper, you can put them on your refrigerator or bulletin board. If you use real stones, you can set them on a window ledge. If you make two sets using two different colors, you can use the stones as game pieces for playing tic-tac-toe.

David wrote lots of songs, poems, and prayers. Many of them are found in the Bible in the book of Psalms. Read this verse that David wrote. Write it on a piece of paper. Read it over and over until you know it by heart:

> When I am afraid, I will put my trust in you. (Psalm 56:3)

The Shepherd's Psalm

PSALM 23

I Can Learn These Words
psalm (SAHLM)
guides (GIDES)

The shepherd takes care
of his sheep every day.
He keeps them close by
so they won't run away.

He feeds them each day.
He knows all their needs.
The sheep gladly follow
wherever he leads.

The shepherd guides them.
He always knows best.
He leads them to places
where they can all rest.

The sheep always trust him.
They never have fear.
They know that the shepherd
will always be near.

The shepherd watches
and loves his sheep.
He stays beside them,
awake or asleep.

God loves his children
in much the same way.
He is our Shepherd—
he's with us to stay.

God is the Teacher.
He teaches what's right.
He watches his children
from morning till night.

The Lord keeps us safe.
He shows us he cares.
He loves his children
and hears all our prayers.
So follow the Shepherd—
don't go your own way.
And pray to the Lord,
who guides you each day.

I Can Read These Words

care
follow
safe

I Can Find the Words That Rhyme

needs	best
rest	stay
sheep	asleep
way	leads

I Can Answer These Questions

How is God like a good shepherd to his children?

How are you like a sheep?

I Can Do These Activities

Practice listening to the shepherd's voice. With family or friends, play a game of "telephone." Think of something a shepherd might say to his sheep and whisper it to another player. That person must listen carefully and whisper what he or she heard to the next person in the game. Continue until everyone has a chance to hear the message. The last person repeats the words aloud. Were you good listeners?

To help you think about Psalm 23, make a field of grass for some cotton sheep: Spread potting soil inside a pie tin and cover it with grass seed. Sprinkle another quarter inch of potting soil over the grass seed and water it well. Glue cotton balls around the outer edge of the pan to be the sheep. Look up Psalm 23 in the Bible and choose your favorite verse. Write the words on both sides of a small piece of paper. Decorate the paper by giving it a nice border. Glue it onto the end of a craft stick or popsicle stick and place it in the soil. Water the grass every few days until it begins to grow.

Three Brave Friends

DANIEL 1; 3

I Can Learn These Words
praise (PRAZE)
statue (STAT-choo)
flutes (FLOOTS)
furnace (FERN-iss)
wrap (RAP)
fiery (FI-er-ee)

I Can Say These Names
Shadrach (SHAD-rack)
Meshach (ME-shack)
Abednego (uh-BED-neh-go)

Three brave friends
did what was right.
They worked for the king
from morning till night.
They always obeyed
the Lord above.
They gave to him
their praise and love.

The king made a statue
ninety feet high.
It reached way up,
so high in the sky.
The statue was big
and covered with gold.
"You must bow down!"
the people were told.
"You'll hear the sound
of pipes and flutes,
of harps and horns
with their root-a-toot-toots.
Then you must bow
and you must pray
to my statue of gold.
You must obey!"

The sound of music
rang through the air.
The people bowed down
to the statue in prayer.
But three brave friends
stood straight and tall.
They didn't bow down
to the statue at all.

The king said, "I'm mad!
I'm madder than mad!
You'd better obey me,
or things will get bad.
Into the furnace
is where we will throw
Shadrach, Meshach,
and Abednego!"

The three friends said,
"We'll never bow
to your statue of gold,
no way, no how!
We only pray
to God above.
He is the one
we choose to love."

The king cried out,
"Turn up the fire!
Make all the flames
hotter and higher!
Wrap them with ropes.
Make sure they're tied.
Open the furnace.
Throw them inside!"

The three friends went in.
The hot fire blazed.
But soon that king
was quite amazed!
Three men went through
the furnace door.
God sent an angel,
and now there were four!

The king could not
believe his eyes.
The men were alive!
What a surprise!
"Come out!" said the king.
"Come right away!
The Lord your God
has saved you today."

The three brave friends
came out the door.
They looked the same
as they had before.
Their skin was fine.
Their hair was too.
The clothes they wore
looked just like new.

The king cried out,
"Give God the praise!
He saved you from
the fiery blaze!
Your God's the greatest
God that I know,
Shadrach, Meshach,
and Abednego."

I Can Read These Words

friends
bow
flames

I Can Find the Words That Rhyme

mad	four
blaze	bad
door	toots
flutes	praise

I Can Answer These Questions

What did the king order everyone to do?

Why did Shadrach, Meshach, and Abednego say they would not obey the king?

What do you think you would have done if you were one of the three friends?

I Can Do These Activities

Use a white paper plate to make a clock. Write the numbers one through twelve around the rim of the plate to make the numbers on the clock. On heavy paper, draw two arrows with one round end and one pointed end. Then cut them out. Ask a grown-up to help you punch a tiny hole in the center of the plate and at the round end of each arrow. Put a paper fastener through the holes at the ends of the arrows and then through the hole in the center of the plate. Allow the hands to turn around the face of the clock. On the back of the clock, make a list of times throughout the day when you can pray to God. Write something you can pray about at each time. For example:

8:00 a.m.: I can thank God for a new day.

12:00 noon: I can thank God for my lunch.

Each time you pray, show what time it is on your clock by moving the arrows to the right numbers.

On a piece of paper, copy the blanks as they appear below so you can fill in the letters for three different words.
___ ___ ___   ___ ___   ___ ___ ___ ___ ___ .

Starting with the letter G, write every other letter from the list below, in order, into the blanks. Once all the blanks have been filled in, you will find out a fact about God.
G T O M D W I B S F G K R P E H A G T

Daniel and the Lions

DANIEL 6

King Darius was
a pretty good king.
He usually tried
to do the right thing.
But he had some helpers
who weren't very nice.
They went to the king
with bad advice.
"Oh King!" said his men.
"You are great and cool!
You should lead forever
and make a new rule.
For the next thirty days,
no person should pray,
except to you,
or be hurt right away!"

King Darius liked
this rule a lot.
So he made it a law
and signed on the spot.
"No one should pray
to anyone but me!
Or the lions' den
is where you will be!"

Daniel loved the Lord.
He prayed three times a day.
He knew what was right.
This rule was not okay.
So Daniel asked God,
"Lord, what should I do?"
He prayed every day,
"Oh Lord, I love you."

The king's evil men
saw Daniel pray.
They said to the king,
"That man has to pay!
Daniel's done wrong!
We've seen him pray.
He's praying to God
three times every day."

The king was upset.
"Oh, what should I do?"
"Stop him!" they said.
"To your law be true!"

The king was so sad.
He knew it was cruel.
But he punished Daniel
for breaking the rule.
Into the lions' den
Daniel was thrown.
He spent the night
in that den all alone.

The king couldn't sleep,
not one little bit.
What happened to Daniel
in that lions' pit?
"Rrrroar! Chomp! Growl!"
said lions in the den.
"Rrrroar! Chomp! Growl!"
went the lions once again.

Early in the morning
the king ran to see—
was Daniel alive?
He hoped it could be.
The king was surprised!
Daniel was okay!
He said, "God was with me
as he is every day.
The Lord sent an angel
to stay here with me.
The lions' jaws were closed
as tight as could be!"

The king told the people,
"Here's what you should do—
worship Daniel's God.
He will take care of you!

"He is Lord of all!
Please listen, my friends.
He will rule forever.
His Kingdom never ends!"

I Can Read These Words

pray
lions
jaws

I Can Find the Words That Rhyme

pit   ends
rule   day
friends   bit
okay   cool

I Can Answer These Questions

Why do you think the king's helpers knew that Daniel would still pray to God after the king made his rule?

How did God keep Daniel safe? Can you think of times when God kept you safe?

I Can Do These Activities

Make a lion mask from a paper plate. Color the lion's face and cut out holes for the eyes. Curl strips of yellow and brown paper by rolling them around a pencil or pen. Then glue the strips of paper around the edges to make the mane. What words might the lions say to Daniel if they could talk?

Daniel knew how important it is to pray. Use some of the words you have learned and write a short prayer to God. What can you thank him for? What do you need God's help with?

Jonah's Big Adventure

JONAH 1–4

I Can Learn These Words
adventure (add-VENN-chur)
captain (CAP-tin)
sailors (SALE-ers)
overboard (OH-ver-bored)

I Can Say This Name
Jonah (JOE-nuh)

I Can Say This Place
Nineveh (NIN-uh-vuh)

Jonah was a prophet.
God said to him one day,
"Tell the folks in Nineveh
I want them to obey.
The people will not listen.
The people make me sad.
They do the things they shouldn't.
They're really very bad!"

But Jonah did not listen.
Oh, no, he ran away!
He hopped onto a ship
and left that very day.

A great big storm blew in.
The ship rocked up and down.
The captain said, "Hey, Jonah!
I think we're going to drown."

Jonah said, "I tried to run
away from God and hide.
I jumped upon this big old boat
and caused this stormy ride."
The lightning CRACKED!
The thunder BOOMED!
"The storm's a sign for me."
Jonah told the captain,
"Just throw me in the sea!"

And so the sailors did it.
They tossed him overboard.
"Oh, please don't let us die!"
they cried out to the Lord.

Down, down, down sank Jonah.
A giant fish came by.
But God was good to Jonah
and did not let him die.
The fish swam right toward Jonah.
Its mouth was open wide.
It took a great big gulp!
Then Jonah was inside.

He prayed inside the fish.
He prayed with all his might.
"Thank you, God, for saving me.
I'll try to do what's right."

Jonah was inside the fish
for three days in a row.
Then the fish swam to the shore.
God told it where to go.

When Jonah looked around,
there wasn't any doubt.
He felt the sand and saw the sky.
The fish had spit him out!
God gave Jonah one more chance
to listen and obey.
He said, "Now go to Nineveh."
So Jonah went that day.

Jonah shouted loudly
to everyone in town,
"Because you've disobeyed the Lord,
your city will come down."
The people were so sorry.
They changed their evil ways.
So God forgave the people,
and they gave God their praise.

I Can Read These Words

ship
sank
fish

I Can Find the Words That Rhyme

drown	out
day	down
Lord	obey
doubt	overboard

I Can Answer These Questions

What did God tell Jonah to do? What are some things that you know God wants you to do?

What happened to Jonah when he did not obey?

I Can Do These Activities

Look at the lists of words on the next page. Which things will help you go from one place to another? On a piece of paper, draw two lines to make a road or path, and write those words on it.

box	train	scooter	bed	hat
shirt	go cart	blanket	row boat	airplane
sled	lamp	tractor	golf cart	paper
ship	car	pan	pillow	horse
bike	flower	bus	TV	van

Now look at all the words again. Which things could help you when you're playing hide-and-seek? Draw a box on the piece of paper and write those words in it. How many things are written on the road or path? How many things are written in the box? Do you think you can run away from God or hide from him? Why or why not?

Draw a picture of a fish on a big piece of paper. Use as much of the paper as you can. Then cut out the fish. Trace the fish onto another piece of paper and then cut it out so that you have two fish that are the same. Glue or staple the two fish together around the outer edges only, leaving the mouth of the fish open. Write this verse on a piece of paper:

> I am always with you; you hold me by my right hand. (Psalm 73:23, NIV)

Put this piece of paper inside the mouth of your fish. Write some other Bible verses on pieces of paper and put them in your fish's mouth too. Pull out these verses when you need to remember that God is with you and that you can never run away from him.

New Testament

"He'll be called Immanuel
and save people from their sins.
You will name him Jesus
when his life on earth begins."

Then Caesar made a rule
that everyone must go
back to his home town—
and no one could say no.
Joseph was from Bethlehem,
far from where they were.
So he brought his wife along
and took good care of her.

The time was very close
for Mary to give birth.
They traveled very far
across the dusty earth.
When at last they got
to Bethlehem one night,
the inns were all too full.
Would Mary be all right?

One man told them kindly,
"My inn is full today.
But you may use my stable
and rest upon the hay."
Chickens peeped, the cow said, "Moo,"
and "Baa" came from the sheep,
while Joseph and dear Mary
both tried to get some sleep.

And when the right time came
for Mary to give birth,
she wrapped her baby boy in cloths.
God's Son was here on earth!

In the fields nearby,
watching sheep that night,
the shepherds saw an angel.
Oh, what an awesome sight!

The angel said, "I have good news!
A baby born today
is lying in a manger
upon a bed of hay."
A group of angels filled the sky
and then began to sing.
"Glory in the highest
to the newborn King!
Let's give praise to God above
for all the love he'll bring!"

The shepherds were excited!
Could this baby be
the promised Savior of the world?
They couldn't wait to see!
The shepherds found the child
just like the angel said,
sleeping in a stable,
tucked in his manger bed.

After baby Jesus came,
some wise men traveled far
to see the little baby born
beneath a shining star.
They came from very far away.
It took them many days.
They longed to see the newborn King
and bow to him in praise.
The star shone brightly in the sky,
showing them the way.
It led them straight to Jesus.
They thanked the Lord that day.

The wise men said to Jesus,
"Please take these gifts we bring—
frankincense and gold and myrrh—
all for the special King."

No need to wait for Christmas
to celebrate his birth.
Happy Birthday, Jesus!
And peace to all the earth!

I Can Read These Words

wife
save
peace

I Can Find the Words That Rhyme

birth	earth
were	far
star	bring
King	her

I Can Answer These Questions

A stable is like a barn. Why was Jesus born there?

Who sent the shepherds to find the baby Jesus? How would you have felt if you heard a message like that?

I Can Do These Activities

Jesus' birth was a wonderful miracle, and you are one of God's miracles too! Grab some friends or family members to play this game. Pass around five small pieces of paper to each person. Write down one word that describes something special about you and one word that describes something special about Jesus on your piece of paper. One person can collect the papers and read each set of words aloud while the rest of the players guess who is being described.

Make a birthday cake for Jesus—on paper. Draw the cake on a piece of paper and color it in, but leave room to write some words. If Jesus came to your house this Christmas to celebrate with you, what gifts do you think he would like to get? Write them on his birthday cake. Now bake Jesus a real cake and enjoy it to remember his birth!

Jesus at the Temple

LUKE 2:41-52

When Jesus was a boy,
he grew bigger every day.
He learned to walk and talk.
He learned to run and play.

When he was twelve years old,
his family took a trip.
They didn't drive a car
or hop onto a ship.
They went with lots of people.
They walked a long, long ways.
The road was dry and dusty.
It took them many days.

They finally reached the Temple.
People came from far away.
The whole town came together
for a special holiday.
The parents talked and ate.
The kids ran here and there.
Everyone gave thanks to God
for all his love and care.

The people went back home.
Again, the trip was long.
Then Mary had a feeling
that something had gone wrong.

Mary said to Joseph,
"Where did Jesus go?"
They asked so many people,
but no one seemed to know.
They looked and looked for Jesus
all through the noisy crowd.
"Has anyone seen Jesus?"
Mary called out loud.

For three long days they searched.
What happened to their son?
They looked and prayed and hoped.
They talked to everyone.

They went back to the Temple
and finally found him there.
Mary said to Jesus,
"We've been looking everywhere!
We thought that you were lost.
I'm worried, can't you see?"
Jesus said, "I wish you'd known
that this is where I'd be."

Jesus met with teachers.
He talked about God's Word.
The teachers were amazed
at everything they heard.

Mary did not understand
the things that Jesus said.
But she kept them in her heart.
She kept them in her head.

Jesus went back home again.
He grew in strength and size.
Everyone was quite amazed
that he could be so wise.

I Can Read These Words

talk
road
town

I Can Find the Words That Rhyme

trip   wise
crowd   heard
word   loud
size   ship

I Can Answer These Questions

Why did Jesus and his family go to the Temple?

What was Jesus doing when his family started going home? Have you ever been separated from your family before? How did you feel?

I Can Do These Activities

In this story, Jesus was twelve years old. How old are you? If you were one of the other kids at the holiday celebration with Jesus, what do you think you would talk about with him? Write one question you would ask Jesus if he lived on earth today.

The Temple that Jesus and his family went to is a little like the churches that people go to today. Do you go to church? If so, find a piece of paper and draw a picture of what your church looks like. What are some things you like to do at church?

John the Baptist

MATTHEW 3

I Can Learn These Words
messenger (MESS-in-jur)
baptize (BAP-tize)
joyfully (JOY-fuh-lee)

I Can Say These Names
John (JON) the Baptist (BAP-tist)
Isaiah (eye-ZAY-uh)
Spirit (SPEAR-it)

John the Baptist
was a good man.
He came one day.
It was God's plan.

Isaiah knew.
He wrote it down.
"A messenger
will come to town.
He'll tell the world
what they must hear.
The time has come.
The Savior's near!"

John came to teach
and baptize, too.
He shared God's love
and spoke what's true.
"Say you're sorry
when you're wrong!
Love the Lord
your whole life long.
Trust in God.
Obey his Word.
Do these things
that you have heard."

John walked around
and liked to wear
clothing made
from camel's hair.
He did not make
a lot of money.
He ate big bugs
with wild honey.

213

The people who
had come to see
John teach God's Word
left joyfully.
Still others asked,
"Who is this man?
What is his name?
What is his plan?"

John kept preaching
every day.
He said, "God wants
you to obey.
After me
a person who
has much more power
will come to you."

Then Jesus came
from Galilee.
He said to John,
"Please baptize me."
But John said, "No!
This cannot be.
For you, my Lord,
should baptize me."
But Jesus said,
"It must be done.
You will baptize
God's own Son."

John was glad
he could obey.
He baptized Jesus
on that day.
Then John looked up
into the sky.
The heavens opened
way up high.

216

John saw God's Spirit
like a dove,
full of power
and full of love.
God said, "This is
my only Son,
who brings more joy
than anyone!"

217

I Can Read These Words

plan
sorry
joy

I Can Find the Words That Rhyme

wear	love
money	me
be	hair
dove	honey

I Can Answer These Questions

What did John do when Jesus came to see him?

John the Baptist was a messenger—he had something to tell people. What was the message he told people about Jesus? What message can YOU tell people about Jesus?

I Can Do These Activities

Here is a game for two or more people. Think of five sets of words you have been learning to rhyme. (Hint: Look at the section called "I Can Find the Words That Rhyme" at the end of each story.) Write each word on a different index card. Make sure each word on a card has a rhyming word on another card. Separate the cards into two piles, making sure each rhyming pair is split up. Shuffle each set of cards, and place them face down on the floor in two piles. Choose one card from each pile. If you have a rhyming match, you get to keep those cards and put them off to the side. If you are wrong, put the cards back in the pile you got each from. Then reshuffle the piles and let another player take a turn. Keep playing until all the cards have been matched up.

John the Baptist ate foods from nature like seeds and bugs. Use glue to write a word from the story on a paper plate. Then cover the glue with sunflower seeds or dried beans and peas. You may also enjoy making a picture using seeds, beans, and peas.

Fishermen Follow Jesus

LUKE 4–6

I Can Learn These Words
lame (LAME)
mute (MYOOT)
leprosy (LEP-ruh-see)
healed (HEELD)
fishermen (FISH-er-men)

I Can Say These Names
Peter (PEET-er)
James (JAYMES)
Andrew (ANN-drew)
Bartholomew (bar-THAH-luh-myoo)
Philip (FILL-ip)
Simon (SIGH-muhn)
Matthew (MATH-you)
Judas (JUDE-us)
Thomas (TOM-us)

When Jesus traveled here and there,
the people came from everywhere.
Some were lame—they could not walk.
Some were mute—they could not talk.
Some were blind—they could not see.
Some were sick with leprosy.

Jesus touched them one by one.
The mute could speak. The lame could run.
He helped the blind so they could see.
He healed those sick with leprosy.

This news of Jesus filled the land:
"He heals the sick by his command.
Come and see what he can do!"
So grown-ups came, and children, too.
They followed Jesus to the shore,
where Jesus taught and healed some more.

Then Jesus met some fishermen.
He said, "Go fishing once again.
Throw your nets into the deep.
You'll catch more fish than you can keep."

A man named Peter shook his head.
"We've fished and fished all night," he said.
"I think the fish all swam away.
But I will do just what you say."

Then right before his very eyes,
Peter saw a great surprise.
Fish were flopping here and there.
Fish were flopping everywhere!
He filled his net up to the top.
They flipped and flopped and would not stop!

Peter waved and gave a shout,
"Hey, fishermen, come help me out!"
They filled their boats and rowed to shore.
They'd never caught so much before!
Then Jesus said, "Come follow me,
and leave your boats beside the sea."

Peter knew just what to do.
He said, "Yes, Lord, I'll follow you!"
James and John did just the same.
When Jesus called, these brothers came.

Later on, a few more men
joined the group, so there were ten.
Andrew and Bartholomew,
Philip, Simon, Matthew too,
Judas and Judas (there were two),
These men all said, "We'll follow you."

Jesus wanted twelve in all.
Two more men obeyed the call:
Thomas and another James.
These were all his helpers' names.

I Can Read These Words

speak
nets
helpers

I Can Find the Words That Rhyme

walk	top
stop	talk
names	command
land	James

I Can Answer These Questions

How many people did Jesus choose to be his helpers? In what ways are you a good helper?

Why did so many people follow Jesus wherever he went? Do you think you would have followed him? Why or why not?

I Can Do These Activities

Look back at the story and read the names of Jesus' helpers. Write their names on a piece of paper. Some of the names are long, so take your time. After you write the names, write your name on the paper also. Jesus wants you to follow him too!

Do you know someone who is sick? Is there someone in your church or neighborhood who can't go many places? Jesus helped many people who were sick or hurting. Make someone a card, and let the person know you are praying for him or her.

Jesus Teaches the People

MATTHEW 5:1-12

Jesus climbed a mountain.
He had a lot to say.
People came to listen.
They came a long, long way.

"Blessed are the poor.
The Kingdom will be theirs.
So if you have no money,
just trust in God who cares.

"Blessed are the people
whose hearts are very sad.
God will love and comfort them
so they won't feel so bad.

"Blessed are the humble
and those who really care.
All the earth will soon be theirs,
a gift from God to share.

"Blessed are the people
who want to do what's right.
God will always hear their prayers.
They're special in his sight.

"Blessed are the kind in heart,
those who can forgive.
In turn, they'll be forgiven,
and they'll forever live.

"Blessed are the people
whose hearts and minds are pure.
Someday up in heaven
they'll see God, that's for sure!

"Blessed are the people
who work for peace each day.
They'll be called God's children
because they work and pray.

"Blessed are the people
who turn the other cheek.
They stand up for the Word of God.
They're not afraid to speak.
They will be rewarded.
Heaven is their prize.
Someday they'll be noticed,
for God will hear their cries.

"Blessed are the people
put to any test.
When they're hurt or being teased,
they give the Lord their best.
They still have faith and joy,
and their reward is great.
Heaven will be waiting,
and it will be first rate!"

Jesus taught these lessons,
meant for you and me.
So we can be the people
that he wants us to be.

I Can Read These Words

people
poor
work

I Can Find the Words That Rhyme

pure	sure
cheek	best
test	cries
prize	speak

I Can Answer These Questions

To be blessed means to have God do wonderful things for us. What kinds of people does God bless? What are some of the ways God blesses you?

What are some of the rewards or gifts that God gives to people who do what Jesus teaches?

I Can Do These Activities

Look through a newspaper or a magazine and try to find a story about someone who did what was right or is a good example to others. Circle words in the story that tell good things about the person.

Go on a treasure hunt! See if you can find:

1. something you can give to the poor
2. something you can give to someone who is sad
3. someone who is loving and caring
4. a rule or direction
5. something with a cross on it
6. a heart or something with a heart on it
7. something that shows peace, like a picture of a dove
8. someone who is praying
9. a Bible
10. a get-well card you can send

When you have found all these things, read the words from the story that go with each one.

Jesus Calms the Storm

LUKE 8:22-56

I Can Learn This Word
trembled (TREM-bulled)

Jesus told his helpers,
"I'm going for a ride.
Let's sail across the lake
to reach the other side."

They climbed inside the boat
and left the sandy shore.
They sailed a little farther.
And then they sailed some more.
They sailed out to the middle.
The lake was getting deep.
Jesus was so tired
that soon he fell asleep.

A storm came on the water.
The winds began to blow.
While Jesus kept on sleeping,
his friends tried hard to row.
The waves were crashing harder.
The boat was tossed about.
"I hope we don't tip over!"
the men began to shout.

The rain was pouring harder
as lightning filled the sky.
The men said to each other,
"I'm sure that we will die!"
The men cried out to Jesus,
"Help! We're going to drown!
We really are in danger.
Our boat is going down!"

Then Jesus asked his helpers,
"Why are you afraid?"
Jesus told the storm to stop.
At once, the storm obeyed!
The men were filled with wonder.
They said, "How can this be?
This Jesus has the power
to calm the wind and sea!"

They sailed again for hours.
They reached the other side.
They saw a man who needed help.
He trembled and he cried.
Jesus loved this man so much.
He helped him on that day.
The people did not like it.
They said, "Please go away."

So Jesus and his helpers
got in the boat once more.
They sailed across the lake again
to where they were before.
The people on the shore
were glad that Jesus came.
He healed a lot of people.
He did it in God's name.

I Can Read These Words

lake
storm
hope

I Can Find the Words That Rhyme

ride   obeyed
came   about
afraid   name
shout   side

I Can Answer These Questions

Why do you think Jesus' helpers were so afraid? How do you think you would have felt if you had been on the boat?

What did Jesus do when his helpers woke him up in the middle of the storm?

I Can Do These Activities

Use some crayons and paper to make a picture of a lake in the middle of a storm. Draw big waves in the water, and clouds and rain. After you make this picture, turn the paper over. Now make a picture of the lake after Jesus told the storm to stop. Draw the lake so it is smooth and calm after the wind and rain stopped. (Make sure the lake is in the same place on both sides of the paper.) Next, cut a slit in the middle of your paper that goes across the top of the water. (Do not cut it all the way to the ends of your paper.) On another piece of paper, make a small boat and cut it out. Tape or glue the boat to the end of a craft stick or straw. Slip the boat through the slit on your paper. As you tell the story to a friend or to someone in your family, show how the boat moves through the water when it is stormy and when it is calm.

On a piece of paper, copy the blanks as they appear below so you can fill in the letters for seven different words.

_ _ _   _ _ _ _ _   _ _ _   _ _ _ _ _

_ _ _ _   _ _ _   _ _ _ _.

Use this code to write something the story can teach us. Write the letters in the blanks on your piece of paper.

A	B	C	D	E	F	G	H	I	J	K	L	M
1	2	3	4	5	6	7	8	9	10	11	12	13

N	O	P	Q	R	S	T	U	V	W	X	Y	Z
14	15	16	17	18	19	20	21	22	23	24	25	26

$\overline{20}\ \overline{8}\ \overline{5}$ $\overline{23}\ \overline{9}\ \overline{14}\ \overline{4}\ \overline{19}$ $\overline{1}\ \overline{14}\ \overline{4}$ $\overline{23}\ \overline{1}\ \overline{22}\ \overline{5}\ \overline{19}$

$\overline{15}\ \overline{2}\ \overline{5}\ \overline{25}$ $\overline{20}\ \overline{8}\ \overline{5}$ $\overline{12}\ \overline{15}\ \overline{18}\ \overline{4}$.

A Boy Shares His Food

JOHN 6:1-15

I Can Learn These Words
hungry (HUNG-gree)
loaves (LOHVZ)
miracle (MEER-uh-kull)

The crowds followed Jesus
as he tried to go and pray.
But when he saw the people,
he couldn't turn away.
And so he healed the sick.
He taught them right from wrong.
He helped so many people,
and the day was getting long!

Jesus told his helpers,
"Please get this crowd some lunch.
The people are so hungry.
There's nothing they can munch."
But Philip said to Jesus,
"Even eight full months' of pay
would never be enough
to feed them all today!"

Andrew said, "I found a boy
who wants to share his snack.
He says he has some food to eat.
It's right inside his sack.
He only has two fish
and five small loaves of bread.
We have so many people.
How can they all be fed?"

Jesus told his helpers,
"Tell everyone around
to find a place where they can sit,
somewhere upon the ground."
At least five thousand people
were in the crowd that day,
and all of them were hungry!
Then Jesus said, "Let's pray."
He broke the little loaves in half,
and then he bowed his head.
He said, "We want to thank you, God,
for all this fish and bread."

His helpers passed out all the food
after Jesus' prayer.
The food just kept on coming—
but they didn't know from where!

"Pick up all the food that's left,"
Jesus finally said.
"Do not waste a single thing.
Find all the fish and bread."
His helpers filled twelve baskets
with food that no one ate.
Jesus can do anything—
because our Lord is great!

"This is quite a miracle!"
the people shouted out.
"Jesus is the Prophet
we've heard so much about."

When Jesus finished teaching,
he left and went away.
He needed time to talk to God
and find a place to pray.

I Can Read These Words

feed
boy
share

I Can Find the Words That Rhyme

lunch   ate
bread   munch
great   snack
sack   said

I Can Answer These Questions

What kind of food did Jesus use to feed all the people? If
you had been listening to Jesus teach the crowd that day,
would you have shared your food? Why or why not?

How much food did Jesus' helpers start with? How much
food was left when they were done?

I Can Do These Activities

Go through old magazines or newspaper ads and cut out pictures of different foods you like to eat. Glue them onto a piece of construction paper, the inside of a box cover, or a piece of felt. Write the name of each food below the picture. Hang it up as a reminder that God blesses you with food for your body, and don't forget to thank God before each meal.

Make pass-it-on cards to share with others. Write these words on several index cards: "You're special! Pass it on!" Decorate each card using markers, stickers, ribbon, or anything else to make it special. Attach a little treat, such as a piece of candy, a cookie, or a sticker. Then share each one with someone special!

Jesus Walks on Water

MATTHEW 14:22-33

Jesus went up
to the hills to pray.
So little by little
the crowds went away.
Jesus' helpers
went away too.
Jesus had told them
just what to do.
He said, "Get your boat
and row out to sea.
Go on ahead.
Don't wait for me."

They got in their boat
and started to row.
But then a strong wind
began to blow.
The wind blew harder.
The waves were high.
The men were afraid
that they would die.

The boat rocked up.
The boat rocked down.
The men were sure
that they would drown.

Then someone cried out,
"What's that I see?
It looks like a ghost!
He's coming toward me!
He's walking on water
and getting too near."
The other helpers
just cried out in fear.

Then Jesus called out,
"Don't fear, it is I!"
The men were so happy
they let out a cry.
Then Peter said, "Lord,
if it really is true,
tell me to come.
I'll walk right to you."

Jesus said, "Peter,
it really is me!
Come over here
and walk on the sea."
So Peter obeyed.
He felt very brave.
He stepped off the boat
and onto a wave.

He walked on the water.
Then something went wrong.
Peter got scared.
The wind was so strong.

"Help me! I'm sinking!"
Peter cried out.
Jesus said, "Peter,
why do you doubt?"
He grabbed Peter's hand.
"My Lord!" Peter cried.
They walked to the boat
and both got inside.

Then all of a sudden,
the wind stopped its roar.
The waves became calm.
The boat shook no more.

The men in the boat
were sure as can be
that only God's Son
was Lord of the sea.
They saw with their eyes
what Jesus had done.
They all said to Jesus,
"You are God's Son!"

I Can Read These Words

wind
rocked
calm

I Can Find the Words That Rhyme

wave	cry
roar	fear
I	more
near	brave

I Can Answer These Questions

What made Peter afraid when he was walking on the water toward Jesus?

What did Jesus do when Peter started sinking? Has Jesus ever helped you when you were afraid?

I Can Do These Activities

Draw a picture of Jesus standing up. Color it, then cut it out. On another piece of paper, use a blue crayon to make a picture of the sea. Glue the picture of Jesus onto the sea so that it shows Jesus walking on the water.

This sentence is written backward. Get out a piece of paper. Then starting with the letter J at the end of the sentence, write down the letters to turn it around and see what is says:

DOG FO NOS EHT SI SUSEJ

Help Your Neighbor

LUKE 10:25-37

I Can Learn These Words
neighbor (NAY-burr)
priest (PREEST)
refused (ree-FYOOZD)
wounded (WOON-ded)
knocked (NAHKT)
thoughtful (THOT-full)

I Can Say This Name
Samaritan (suh-MARE-uh-tin)

"Please tell me, who's my neighbor?"
A man sure wanted to know.
So Jesus told this story
a long, long time ago.

One day a man was walking.
Some robbers were nearby.
They stole his money, beat him up,
and left him there to die.
Soon a priest came down the road
along that very way.
The hurt man cried, "Please help me!"
But the priest refused to stay.
A little while later,
another person passed.
The hurt man cried, "Please help me!
I need you. Please come fast!"

But this man looked the other way.
He left him right there too.
He turned his head and walked away.
What do you think YOU'D do?

Then a good Samaritan,
from another town,
found the wounded, helpless man
and saw he'd been knocked down.
He knew he had to help this man.
He chose to lend a hand.
He cleaned and bandaged up the cuts,
then helped the man to stand.

He took him to a nearby inn,
a place where he could stay.
Whatever it would cost the man,
he promised he would pay.
"If it should cost more money,
I'll give you what you need."
His heart was full of kindness
when he did this thoughtful deed.

Then Jesus asked this question:
"Please tell me, if you can,
which one was the neighbor
to the helpless, wounded man?"

The man who heard the story
answered right away.
He said, "It was the one who stopped
to help the man that day."

Jesus knew he understood.
He said, "Your answer's right.
Now go and do as he did.
This is pleasing in God's sight."

Being a good neighbor
means a whole lot more
than just where you are living
or who you meet next door.
It means when someone's hurting,
you stop to help them out.
That's what a good neighbor
is really all about!

I Can Read These Words

help
inn
hurting

I Can Find the Words That Rhyme

by	need
hand	die
deed	stand
ago	know

I Can Answer These Questions

How did the first two men treat the hurt man?

Who stopped to help the hurt man? Why do you think he helped him?

I Can Do These Activities

God wants everyone to be a good neighbor. Being a good neighbor means being kind to everyone—people who live close to you and people who live far away. Who has done something nice for you? Write that person a short note, thanking him or her for that kindness. Then give the person the note.

Answer these questions on a sheet of paper:
1. What is your favorite food?
2. What is your favorite drink?
3. Where do you live?
4. What is your favorite thing to wear?
5. What do you do to feel better when you are sick?
6. What do you do to feel better when you've done something wrong?

Read these sentences from Matthew 25:35-36 and fill in the blanks with the answers from your piece of paper. You will see how Jesus wants you to treat your neighbor.

I was hungry and you gave me _____ (1).

I was thirsty and you gave me _____ (2).

I was a stranger and you invited me to _____ (3).

I needed clothes and you gave me _____ (4).

I was sick and you _____ (5) with me.

I was in prison and you _____ (6) with me.

Now read Matthew 25:37-40. When you help your neighbor, who else is happy?

Two Sad Sisters

JOHN 11:1-45

A man named Lazarus
was so very sick.
His sisters both said,
"Let's find Jesus quick!"
Mary and Martha
and Lazarus, too,
were friends of Jesus.
And all of them knew
that Jesus could heal him
that very same day.
And so they asked Jesus
to come right away.

When Jesus found out,
he said, "There's no hurry.
God has a plan.
We don't have to worry."
Then after two days,
he went off to see
his very good friends
in Bethany.

When Martha saw Jesus,
she said as she cried,
"Lord, you're too late.
Our brother has died.
I wish you had come
as soon as you knew."
Then Mary came out
to see Jesus too.

She fell at his feet
when Jesus came near.
She said, "Oh, my Lord,
I wish you'd been here.
He would have been healed.
But now he is dead."
Then Jesus was sad.
"Where is he?" he said.

They showed him a stone
in front of a cave.
"He's here," said the sisters.
"This is his grave."
The sisters were crying,
and Jesus cried too.
He said, "Move the stone.
That's what we must do."

"Oh no!" Martha said.
"He's been there too long.
The cave will be stinky!
The smell will be strong!"
Jesus said, "Martha,
believe and you'll see
the glory and power
God's given to me.
Your brother will live.
It will happen today."
And so the big stone
was taken away.

Jesus looked up
as he said out loud,
"Father, I'm praying
in front of this crowd.
I know that you hear me
whenever I pray.
I want them to see
your glory today."

Then Jesus called out,
"Lazarus, come here!"
The people all watched
with wonder and fear.
Lazarus came out
wrapped in white clothes,
from the top of his head
to the tips of his toes.

"Unwrap his body,"
the Lord Jesus said.
"Your brother's alive.
He's no longer dead."

Mary and Martha
were no longer sad.
Their brother was living,
and that made them glad.
Their friends were so happy
they jumped up and down.
They talked about Jesus
all over the town.
"We know he's God's Son,"
some of them said.
"It has to be true.
He raises the dead!"

I Can Read These Words

man
sisters
cave

I Can Find the Words That Rhyme

sick   cried
near   strong
died   quick
long   hear

I Can Answer These Questions

Why do you think Jesus waited to go to his friends when he knew Lazarus was sick? Have you ever had to wait a long time for someone?

What happened when Jesus told Lazarus to come out of the grave?

I Can Do These Activities

The white grave clothes that Lazarus wore were probably long strips of cloth wrapped around his body. What do you think he looked like when he came out of the cave? Ask a grown-up if you may use a roll of toilet paper. Then have a friend or family member wrap you up in toilet paper from head to toe. Make sure to leave an opening for your nose so you can breathe. You will look a lot like Lazarus did when he came out of the grave.

Mary and Martha were so happy and thankful that Jesus brought their brother back to life. What are you happy and thankful for today? Write down two or three things that you can thank God for. Then say a prayer and thank God for each of those things.

The Lost Sheep

LUKE 15:1-7

I Can Learn These Words
sinners (SIN-erz)
flock (FLAHK)
rejoice (ree-JOYSS)

When Jesus taught the people,
many came to hear.
But not all of the people
were happy, that was clear.
The teachers in the Temple
said, "Look how Jesus acts!
He hangs around with sinners.
Yes, those are all the facts."

Do you think that shepherd
would leave his great big flock
to go and find the lost one
and search behind each rock?
Yes! He went out searching.
He looked both far and wide
until he found the lost sheep
and brought it to his side.

When the shepherd found it,
back behind a rock,
he put it on his shoulders
and returned it to the flock.

He called his friends and neighbors
and said, "Let's celebrate!
I found the sheep that had been lost.
Isn't that just great?"

Then Jesus said, "I tell you this,
heaven will rejoice
when just one sinner turns from sin
and makes a godly choice.
There will be a party,
even for just one.
When a sinner comes to Jesus,
his new life has begun!"

I Can Read These Words

story
lost
found

I Can Find the Words That Rhyme

acts   flock
rejoice   facts
rock   begun
one   choice

I Can Answer These Questions

Why do you think the shepherd would leave ninety-nine sheep to search for just one that was lost?

How is the shepherd in the story like Jesus?

I Can Do These Activities

Create a sheep snack by dipping marshmallows into whipped topping or marshmallow creme. Then roll the marshmallows in crispy rice cereal. Place four narrow pretzel sticks into the bottom of each marshmallow for the legs. If sheep could talk, what do you think they might say when they are lost? What might they say when they are found by their shepherd? Enjoy your snack!

Play a lost-and-found game. Ask a friend or family member to place ten items on a tray and cover them with a towel. When you're ready, have them take off the towel. Spend thirty seconds looking at all the items before they are covered again. Then list each item you remember on a piece of paper. How did you do? Next, ask the other person to remove one item from the tray. Can you figure out which item is missing?

The Son Who Left Home

LUKE 15:11-32

I Can Learn These Words
foolish (FOO-lish)
servants (SERVE-unts)
sandals (SAND-ulls)

A son said to his father,
"I'm leaving home today.
I want to see the country
and travel far away."
His father gave him money.
He said, "I'll miss you so!
Remember that I love you.
Be careful where you go."

The son thought he was happy
and everything was fine.
He spent a lot of money
on food and friends and wine.
But all his wild living
and parties did not last.
The son was very foolish.
He spent his money fast.

His friends said, "See you later!
We have no time for you."
The son was sad and lonely.
He wondered what to do.
He worked hard for a farmer
and fed pigs all day long.
The son began to understand
his actions were all wrong.

He said, "My father's servants
are better off than I.
Perhaps my dad will hire me.
At least I ought to try."

He went to see his father,
who met him on the way.
His father said, "My son is home!
Oh, what a happy day!"

The son said, "I'm so sorry!
I should not be your son.
I hope you can forgive me
for everything I've done."
The father did forgive him.
He hugged his son so tight.
And so the son knew right away
that things would be all right.

The father gave his son new clothes
and sandals for his feet.
They had a great big fancy feast
with lots of food to eat.

But then the older brother
heard the happy sound.
He saw the people singing
and dancing all around.
The brother said, "What's going on?
And what's with all this food?"
"Your brother's back," the father said.
"We're in a happy mood!"

The brother was not happy.
He would not join the fun.
He said, "I've worked so hard for you.
I've been a better son!"

His father said, "Please listen.
You have been good to me.
But everything I have is yours.
I love you—can't you see?
Your brother has come back to us,
so let's be glad today.
Your brother was alone and lost,
but now he's found his way."

Jesus told this story
so everyone would know
that God wants us to come to him
and that he loves us so.
It makes God very happy
when people do what's right.
When people choose to follow him,
it's pleasing in God's sight.

I Can Read These Words

money
pigs
feast

I Can Find the Words That Rhyme

feet	son
fast	eat
fun	sound
around	last

I Can Answer These Questions

What did the son do after he left home?

How did the father feel when the son came back home?
How is God like the father in the story?

I Can Do These Activities

Draw a picture of a big table with many different kinds of food on it. On your picture, write the names of five different kinds of foods that you like to eat. Be sure to draw those foods in your picture.

Sometimes people make special meals to show other people how much they love them. Some families have special meals to celebrate birthdays or holidays. Think of someone you love and make a special treat for that person. You might want to make a snack of cheese and crackers or graham crackers with peanut butter. After you share your special treat, you can also show your love by playing a game or reading a book together.

People Praise Jesus

MATTHEW 21:1-11

I Can Learn These Words
allow (ull-OW)
hosanna (ho-ZANN-uh)
explained (ex-PLAIND)

I Can Say This Place
Jerusalem (juh-ROO-suh-lem)

While he was on a mountain,
Jesus stopped to show
two of his good helpers
a town where they should go.
"You will find a donkey.
Please bring it back to me.
Tell anyone who asks you,
'It's for the Lord, you see.'
The owner will allow you
to take it right away."
And that's just how it happened,
as he said it would that day.

His helpers went right into town,
and when they looked ahead,
they saw a donkey waiting,
just as Jesus said.
The men brought back the donkey
for Jesus' special ride.
They put a coat upon its back
and walked by Jesus' side.

They came into Jerusalem.
A crowd was waiting there.
They spread their coats for Jesus
and waved branches in the air.

"Hosanna to the Lord!" they cried
and waved their arms about.
"Hosanna in the highest!"
the people shouted out.

Some people in Jerusalem
asked, "Who could this man be?"
Excited crowds explained to them,
"The man from Galilee.
This is Jesus, God's own Son,
a prophet and much more.
Jesus is the Savior
we've all been waiting for."

I Can Read These Words

donkey
coats
branches

I Can Find the Words That Rhyme

me	see
air	out
more	there
about	for

I Can Answer These Questions

What did the people do when they saw Jesus riding into Jerusalem on a donkey?

How might you have shown your love and joy if you had seen Jesus riding into town?

I Can Do These Activities

This is a game you can play with friends or family or by yourself. Name as many words as you can that fit in each group below. To make the game harder, limit yourself to words that begin with the same letter. Allow yourself three minutes for each group. Look back at stories in this book if you need ideas.

- words that describe Jesus
- animals in the Bible
- places in the Bible
- names of people in the Bible
- Jesus' helpers
- foods eaten in the Bible

Have a praise parade for Jesus! Gather together with friends and family members and talk about all the wonderful reasons to praise Jesus. Make a large banner for everyone to write down their reasons. Make the banner from newsprint or felt and write on it with permanent markers or fabric paint. Ask a grown-up to sew or glue a dowel rod to each side of the banner so that two people can hold it for everyone to see during the parade. Make musical instruments and flags, and decorate your bicycles and other riding toys. Sing songs like "Jesus Loves Me" as you march or ride in the parade. Have little candies with an attached Bible verse and an invitation to come to your church that you can give to anyone watching your parade.

Wash Your Feet before You Eat

JOHN 13:1-30;
MATTHEW 26:20-30, 36-44

I Can Learn These Words
squeaky (SQUEEK-ee)
awful (AWE-full)

Jesus and his helpers
were sitting down to eat
when Jesus got some water
to wash his helpers' feet.
Then one by one he washed them.
But Peter said, "Not me!
You should never wash my feet.
That's not how it should be!"

Then Jesus said to Peter,
"It's what I need to do.
Let me wash your dirty feet
so I can be with you."
But Jesus wasn't talking
about the dirt outside.
He wants to wash away the sins
that we all try to hide.
So Peter said, "Wash all of me
until I'm squeaky clean.
Wash my head, my hands, my feet,
and places in between!"

Jesus washed his helpers' feet,
and then when he was through,
he said, "You call me Teacher.
I've shown you what to do.
Please remember what I say
and have a servant's heart.
You should wash each other's feet,
but that is just the start.
Do all the things I've taught you,
and try to do your best.
Just follow what I've shown you,
and you'll be truly blessed."

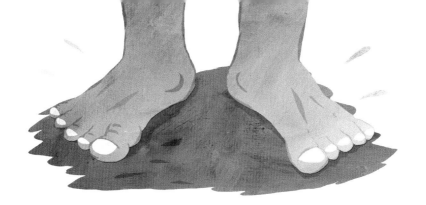

They sat around the table
and ate their food that night.
Jesus said, "I speak the truth.
Something isn't right.
One of you has made a deal,
so now I soon will die."
One by one his helpers said,
"Oh, Lord, it isn't I!"

"Who would do this awful thing?"
his helper Peter said.
Jesus said, "It is the one
who gets this piece of bread."
He gave the bread to Judas,
and Judas went away.
Then Jesus took a loaf of bread
and bowed his head to pray.

He broke the bread in pieces.
He said, "This is for you.
Please take this bread and eat it,
and every time you do,
think about my body
that I'll give up for you."

Jesus took a cup to drink
and thanked the Lord above.
He said, "I'll give my blood for you
to show you all my love.
When you drink this, think of me.
Believe the words I say.
The blood that I pour out for you
will wash your sins away."

Jesus' helpers ate the bread
and had a sip to drink.
Jesus said he soon would die.
They weren't sure what to think.
They went into a garden
and found a quiet spot.
Jesus' helpers fell asleep,
but Jesus prayed a lot.

I Can Read These Words

water
wash
dirt

I Can Find the Words That Rhyme

drink	start
clean	lot
heart	think
spot	between

I Can Answer These Questions

Why do you think Jesus washed his helpers' feet?

What did Jesus want his helpers to remember from their special meal together? What are some ways that you can remember Jesus?

I Can Do These Activities

Take off your socks and shoes and trace both your feet on a piece of paper. Color one tracing of your foot so that it's the color of your foot when it's dirty. Color the other tracing of your foot so it's the color of your foot when it's clean. Then write this Bible verse on the clean tracing of your foot:

> I have given you an example to follow. Do as I have done to you. (John 13:15)

Let these footprints remind you of the time when Jesus washed his helpers' feet. How does Jesus want you to treat others?

Draw a picture of a table. On top of the table, draw a loaf of bread and a cup. Let this picture remind you of the special meal Jesus and his helpers ate together.

Jesus Dies on a Cross

MATTHEW 26:47–27:60; LUKE 23:26-56; JOHN 18–19

I Can Learn These Words
arrested (uh-REST-ed)
confused (ken-FUZED)

I Can Say These Names
Christ (KRYST)
Pilate (PIE-lit)

I Can Say This Place
Gethsemane (Geth-SEM-uh-nee)

In the garden of Gethsemane,
Jesus knelt to pray.
When Judas gave the guards a sign,
some men took him away.
Then Jesus was arrested.
The high priest said, "Tell me,
are you the Christ, the Son of God?"
He answered, "I am he."
Jesus said, "I taught the crowds
but never taught them wrong.
Just ask the ones who listened
to my teachings all day long."

Peter said he'd follow
Jesus till the end.
But when they talked to Peter,
he said, "I'm not his friend."
Three times Peter said this.
"He's not my friend," he lied.
But when he thought about it,
Peter ran away and cried.

The soldiers then took Jesus
to Pilate, who said, "Why?
What has Jesus done that's wrong?
Why should Jesus die?"

The priests all said to Pilate,
"He thinks that he's a King.
He claims to be the Son of God.
We can't have such a thing!"
Then Pilate said to Jesus,
"You say that you're a King?"
Jesus said, "Yes, that is true.
I'm King of everything.
My Kingdom is not of this world.
The reason I am here
is to show that God is love
and make his truth quite clear."

Then Pilate said to all the crowd,
"What will your answer be?
Should Jesus be the one we kill,
or should I set him free?"
The people shouted, "Kill him!"
They'd turned against him now.
So Pilate said, "That's what you want,
so this I will allow."

They dressed up Jesus in a robe.
They laughed at him and said,
"Here's a crown of thorns for you!"
and placed it on his head.
The soldiers beat up Jesus.
They spit into his face.
They were very mean to him,
but he just showed them grace.

They followed Jesus to a hill
where he was going to die.
They nailed him to a wooden cross.
His friends began to cry.

But other people shouted out,
"Save yourself! Come down!
Show us you're the Son of God,
the King who wears the crown!"
Two robbers hung beside him.
One robber said, "Hey, you!
If you're God's Son, then save yourself,
and try to save us, too!"
The other robber shouted,
"Our punishment is fair.
Jesus has done nothing wrong
except to love and care."

Jesus told the second man,
"Today you'll be with me.
Heaven will be waiting
for both of us, you'll see."

Jesus hung upon the cross
and saw his mother cry.
She stood beside his good friend John.
Then Jesus said good-bye.

"Dear woman, this will be your son.
My friend, this is your mother."
From that day on, John took her home.
They cared for one another.

"I'm thirsty!" Jesus cried that day,
as soldiers bet their money.
They threw some dice to get his clothes
and thought all this was funny.

"My God, my God! Why have you left?"
said Jesus with a cry.
Then rocks began to split apart,
and darkness filled the sky.

"It is finished," Jesus said.
He bowed his head and died.
A man on guard was so afraid.
"That IS God's Son!" he cried.
Some friends wrapped Jesus' body.
They placed him in a cave.
They rolled a stone in front of it,
with Jesus in the grave.

I Can Read These Words

truth
just
cross

I Can Find the Words That Rhyme

here	grace
now	allow
face	grave
cave	clear

I Can Answer These Questions

When Pilate asked what should be done with Jesus, what did the people say?

How did the soldiers treat Jesus after they decided he should be killed? Why do you think they did that?

I Can Do These Activities

Write down the name of someone you care about a whole bunch. Now write down the name of someone who has upset you or made you feel bad. Get a box and fill it with little gifts to give to someone you care about. Include things you made, cookies you baked, pretty rocks or beads, stickers, pencils, or other treats. Next, wrap up the gift and make it look as nice as you can. Now give the gift to the person who upset you! Is it hard to give a loving gift to someone who was unkind to you? How is that similar to what Jesus did when he died on the cross?

Look at the words below. Use a dark crayon to color over the words that are sins—things you know are wrong. What do you see when you are done? (Note to parents and teachers: If you'd rather have children do this activity on paper, you can copy this page or have them use tracing paper.)

tease annoy   welcome listen love   break complain
whine steal   praise understand   selfish hit steal
brag selfish   share support care   fight cheat hate
honor value accept honest praise give share trust
serve understand support appreciate forgive obey
ignore attack   believe care love   upset hurt steal
cheat selfish   welcome support   break swear slap
break insult   appreciate accept   injure lie punch
hate hit steal   listen obey praise   selfish slap upset
hurt tease hit   respect praise care   fight annoy lie
whine swear   support give share   cheat hate brag
lie sneak hit   love listen forgive   annoy complain

Jesus Is Alive!

MATTHEW 28:1-10, 16-20; JOHN 20:19-23; LUKE 24:36-41, 50-53

Early Sunday morning,
the ground began to shake.
Two friends whose names were Mary
were already wide awake.
They walked with one another
to the place where Jesus lay.
But when they reached the cave,
the stone was rolled away!

The women saw an angel.
His clothes were very bright.
He sat upon the stone.
The women shook with fright.
"Please don't be afraid,"
the friendly angel said.
"Jesus is not here!
He's risen from the dead."

The women started smiling.
They knew that it was true.
The angel said, "You'll see him soon.
He's gone ahead of you.
Go and tell his helpers
he is alive today."
The women listened to him,
then quickly went away.

The women were so happy.
They ran and ran and ran.
Then someone stopped to say hello.
Who was this friendly man?
They saw that it was Jesus!
He was alive, not dead!
Jesus said, "Don't be afraid.
I'm here, just as I said.
Go and tell my helpers
to go to Galilee.
Tell them I will see them
and they will soon see me."

"We have talked to Jesus!"
the happy women said.
"Jesus is alive today.
He's risen from the dead!"
But when the helpers heard this,
the men began to doubt.
They really did not understand
what this was all about.

They met inside a quiet room
and locked the doors up tight.
Then Jesus stood before them.
The men were filled with fright.

"Peace be with you!" Jesus said.
"Believe and do not fear.
See my hands, my feet, and side?
It's me! I'm really here!"

Then the helpers were not scared
but filled with joy instead.
Now they finally understood
the things that Jesus said.

Then Jesus blessed his helpers.
He said, "Now you must go
and tell the world about me.
Tell everything you know.
Teach them to obey me
and believe my words are true.
I'm giving you this promise:
I'll always be with you."

Then Jesus went to heaven.
And when he went away,
they held on to his promise
and praised him every day.

I Can Read These Words

hello
heaven
praised

I Can Find the Words That Rhyme

awake	said
tight	lay
instead	fright
away	shake

I Can Answer These Questions

What did the angel tell the two friends named Mary when they went to Jesus' cave?

What promise did Jesus make to his helpers when he went up to heaven? How do you feel knowing that Jesus makes the same promise to you?

I Can Do These Activities

Use some paper and crayons to draw and color a picture of the empty cave. Write the words "Jesus is alive!" on the inside of the cave. Draw a big stone on another piece of paper. Make the stone about one inch bigger than the opening of the cave. Place the stone over the opening. Glue the extra inch to the left side of the opening. Then carefully fold the stone to make a flap so it can open and close. Share your picture with family and friends. Let them open the stone so they can see the wonderful message on the inside.

Jesus asked his helpers to tell everyone that he had come back to life. Jesus wants you to share this message with others too! You can share the Good News by making someone a card, writing someone a letter, or making a sign to hang in your house. Can you think of other ways you can tell people that Jesus is alive? Choose at least one of these things to do this week.

A New Follower of Jesus

ACTS 9:1-31

I Can Learn This Word
patiently (PAY-shunt-lee)

I Can Say These Names
Saul (SAWL)
Christians (KRISS-chuns)
Ananias (ann-uh-NYE-us)
Paul (PAWL)

I Can Say This Place
Damascus (duh-MASK-us)

There was a man whose name was Saul.
He hated Christians, one and all.
He tried to hunt them every day.
He wanted them to go away.

He was cruel and so unkind
to any Christians he could find.
Saul was mean and did not care.
He looked for Christians everywhere.
He locked up men and women, too,
if they believed God's words were true.

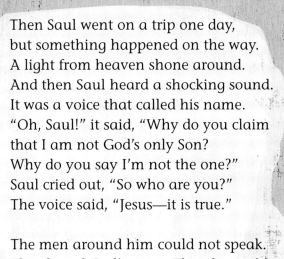

Then Saul went on a trip one day,
but something happened on the way.
A light from heaven shone around.
And then Saul heard a shocking sound.
It was a voice that called his name.
"Oh, Saul!" it said, "Why do you claim
that I am not God's only Son?
Why do you say I'm not the one?"
Saul cried out, "So who are you?"
The voice said, "Jesus—it is true."

The men around him could not speak.
They heard God's voice. Their knees felt weak.
But they could not see anyone
as Saul fell down before God's Son.

Then Jesus said, "Get up and go
right into town, where you will know
just what to do and what to say."
So Saul obeyed him right away.

Then Saul called out, "Hey, friends! Help me!
My eyes are blind. I cannot see!"
His friends helped Saul up from the ground.
He needed help to get around.
For three long days, poor Saul was blind.
He ate no food of any kind.

In Damascus was a man.
He had a dream about God's plan.
"Ananias," God's voice said,
"talk to Saul and touch his head.
He's praying now and soon he'll see
that he was made to follow me."

"I'm afraid!" Ananias cried.
"Saul hates the people on your side."

"Go!" God said. "I chose this man
to work for me. This is my plan.
He'll bring my name to everyone.
He'll teach about my only Son."

So Ananias went to see
where Saul was waiting patiently.
"Hello there, Saul," Ananias said.
"I'll help you see." He touched his head.
"The Holy Spirit lives in you,
so now you'll follow Jesus too."

Then suddenly Saul got his sight.
He knew that trusting God was right.
So Saul was baptized right away.
He gave his heart to God that day.

People were surprised to hear
about this man they used to fear.
Some didn't like this change at all,
but others liked this brand-new Saul!

His name was changed from Saul to Paul.
He boldly preached God's Word to all.
He traveled far and taught God's way.
"Christ is our Lord!" Paul liked to say.
"Jesus loves us and forgives
all of our sins because he lives!"

I Can Read These Words

light
trip
taught

I Can Find the Words That Rhyme

speak   claim
blind   all
name   weak
Paul   kind

I Can Answer These Questions

What happened to Saul when he went on his trip?

What did Saul do after he believed in Jesus? Have you ever
seen a change in someone's life?

I Can Do These Activities

Many people in the Bible had more than one name. How many names do you have? Many people today have a first, middle, and last name. Practice writing your full name. Ask your parents how they chose your name. Then ask your family and friends to tell you their full names and how they were chosen. You may hear some interesting stories!

Paul taught people that Jesus is the only way to God. In John 14:6 (NIV), Jesus says, "I am the way and the truth and the life." Draw a large cross on a piece of paper and cut it out. Write the word WAY on the left side of the cross. Write the word TRUTH on the right side of the cross. Write the word LIFE on the center top of the cross. Talk with your family about what each word teaches you about Jesus.